60 KAGAN STRUCTURES

More Proven Engagement Strategies

Dr. Spencer Kagan
Miguel Kagan
Laurie Kagan

Kagan

Kagan Publishing
981 Calle Amanecer
San Clemente, CA 92673
800.933.2667
www.KaganOnline.com

ISBN: 978-1-933445-58-8

Kagan Structures
QUICK LOOK

60 KAGAN STRUCTURES

TABLE OF CONTENTS

TABLE OF CONTENTS continued

Table of Contents

STRUCTURE FUNCTIONS

This dot chart illustrates recommended uses for the structures featured in this book. The structures here represent a subset of more than 200 Kagan Structures.

60 Kagan Structures

KEY
★ HIGHLY RECOMMENDED
• RECOMMENDED

STRUCTURES

Structure	Page	Classbuilding	Teambuilding	Social Skills	Communication Skills	Decision Making	Knowledgebuilding	Procedure Learning	Processing Info	Thinking Skills	Presentations
		Interpersonal					Academic				
AGREE-DISAGREE LINE-UPS	1	★		★	★	★			•	★	
ANSWER-N-EXPLAIN	17			★	★		★	★			
BLIND FEEDBACK	29			★	★				★	★	
CAROUSEL DISCUSS	28			★	★				★	★	
CAROUSEL FEEDBACK	21			★	★	•			•	★	
CIRCLE-THE-SAGE	35	★		★	★		★	★	★	★	
CONSENSUS SEEKING	43		•	★	★	★			•	★	
CRYSTALLIZE IT!	51	•		★	★	•	•		★	★	
DOUBLE FOLDED LINE-UPS	9	•		★	★						
DROP-A-CHIP	57			★	★						
FIND A DIFFERENT NUMBER	205	★		★							
FIND MY RULE	61			★	★		•		★	★	
FIND YOUR MATCH	206	★		★							
FIND YOUR NUMBER	205	★		★	★						
FIST TO FIVE	73			★	★	★					
FOLDED LINE-UPS	8	•		★	★						
FORMATIONS	77	★		★			★				
INDIVIDUAL WHIP!	274			★	★		•		•	•	•
LISTEN UP!	83			★	★		★		★	★	
LOGIC LINE-UPS	87		•	★	★	•	★	★		★	
LOOK-WRITE-DISCUSS	99			★	★					★	•
MATCH MINE	105			★	★		★			★	
MIX-N-MATCH	117	★		★	★		★		★		
OBSERVE-DRAW-ROUNDROBIN	135			★	★		•			★	
OBSERVE-WRITE-ROUNDROBIN	131		•	★	★		★			★	
OPINION SAGES	40	•		★	★					★	•
OVERLAP MAP	234			★	★		★				
PAIRS COMPARE	137		★	★	★	•	★		•	★	
PAIR STAND-N-SHARE	242			★	★		★		★		★
PARTNER STAR	147			★	★		★			★	

KEY ★ HIGHLY RECOMMENDED · RECOMMENDED

STRUCTURES	Page	Classbuilding	Teambuilding	Social Skills	Communication Skills	Decision Making	Knowledgebuilding	Procedure Learning	Processing Info	Thinking Skills	Presentations
		Interpersonal					Academic				
PICKING STICKIES	151	★		★	★		★		★		
Q & A REVIEW	155			★	★		★	·	★		
RAPPIN' PAIRS	162			★	★		★			★	★
RAPPIN' TEAMS	159			★	★		★			★	★
READ-N-TELL!	165			★	★		★		★	★	
ROVING REPORTER	169			★	★		★		★		★
SAME-DIFFERENT	173			★	★		★	·		★	
SHARE-N-SWITCH	183			★	★		★	★	★	★	
SHOW ME	187			★	★		★	·	★	★	★
SPEND-A-BUCK	193			★	★	★					
SPLIT-N-SLIDE LINE-UPS	7	·		★	★						
STAND-N-SHARE	241			★	★		★	★			
STANDUP-HANDUP-PAIRUP	201	★		★	★		★	·	★	★	·
STEPUP	216	·		★	★	·				★	
SWITCH OR TRADE	209			★	★		★	·	★	★	
TAKEOFF-TOUCHDOWN	213			★	★						
TEAM FORMATIONS	82		★	★			★				
TEAMMATES CONSULT	245		★	★	★		★	·	★	★	
TEAM MIND-MAPPING	217		★	★	★		★		★	★	★
TEAM OVERLAP MAP	231		★	★	★		★		★		
TEAMS COMPARE	142		·	★	★		★		★	★	★
TEAM STAND-N-SHARE	235			★	★		·		·		★
TEAM WORD-WEBBING	223		·	★	★		★		★	★	★
TIMED TRAVELERS	255	★		★	★				★	★	★
TRAVELING PAIR REVIEW	150	★		★	★		★	·	★	★	
TRAVELING STAR	261			★	★		★	·	★	★	
TURN TOSS	265		·	★	★		★		★	★	
WHIP	271			★	★		★		★	★	
WHISPER IT!	243			★	★		★	·			
WHO AM I?	275	★		★	★		★			★	

Structure Functions

60 Kagan Structures
INTRODUCTION

By Dr. Spencer Kagan

STRUCTURES ARE EMPOWERING. They transform teaching and learning. When I think of the power of structures, I think of the power of a well-placed lever. Given the proper lever, with little effort, we can lift a huge load. Structures are like that. With a little effort, we can dramatically increase academic achievement, reduce the achievement gap, improve social and ethnic relations, foster social skills and character, and reduce the incidence and severity of discipline problems. Structures are an educator's dream!

> "Give me a lever long enough and a fulcrum on which to place it, and I shall move the world."
> —Archimedes

Any thoughtful educator should question these claims. How can instructional strategies as simple as **RallyRobin** or **Timed Pair Share** transform teaching and learning? Although each structure fosters specific thinking skills and social skills, the structures all have something in common: They radically increase the amount of active engagement among students. And when students are actively engaged, learning is accelerated.

Let's examine how a simple structure transforms the amount of active engagement. Let's compare the amount of engagement in a traditional classroom with the amount in a classroom using Kagan Structures. After asking a question of the class, the traditional teacher calls on students one at a time to answer. To give a student 1 minute of active engagement—1 minute to verbalize his or her thinking in response to the teacher's question—it takes about 2 minutes. Why? First, the teacher has to ask the question, then the student answers the question, and then the teacher responds to the student's answer. The teacher talks twice for each time the student talks, so it takes about 2 minutes to give a student 1 minute of active verbalization. With approximately 30 students in the class, the best the teacher can do is give each student 1 minute of active engagement per hour!

In contrast, after asking the same question of the class, the teacher uses **RallyRobin** or **Timed Pair Share**, allowing students 2 minutes to interact. In 2 minutes, every student in the class has had a minute of active engagement. Using Kagan Structures, the teacher accomplishes in 2 minutes what the traditional teacher would take an hour to accomplish; Kagan Structures produce 30 times as much active engagement!

RallyRobin and **Timed Pair Share** are just two examples of the many Kagan Structures in this series. They are alternatives to the ever-present traditional question-and-answer sessions. Structures multiply student engagement by unleashing the power of simultaneous student-to-student interaction. All students are engaged at once instead of one at a time. The structures in this book provide alternatives to traditional teaching that escalate student engagement for many different learning objectives, including brainstorming, guided practice, reviews, test preparation, information processing, higher-level thinking, and more. When we use Kagan Structures as a regular part of the way we teach, students' classroom experience is radically transformed. Instead of listening passively or being engaged rarely, full engagement becomes the daily norm. Kagan Structures actively engage all students!

> Why would we want to call on just one student when, in the same amount of time, we could call on all students?

If increasing active engagement were all structures did, it would be enough of a justification to begin teaching with structures. Why? Because students who are not engaged by the traditional classroom structure disengage from schooling. They tune out, fall behind, and when the achievement gap becomes oppressive, drop out. Engagement is like a safety net for the classroom. It catches students who otherwise would fall through the cracks of our traditional educational system. When they are engaged, students learn so much more. The gap between the higher and lower achievers shrinks because the students who could opt to tune out are tuning in with great interest and excitement as they interact with partners, teammates, and classmates over the curriculum. The gap shrinks by engaging the disengaged and bringing the bottom up.

Full student engagement boosts student learning and decreases the achievement gap. But structures do so much more. Kagan Structures build social skills and transform social orientation by creating a more cooperative and caring classroom. When students compete for the teacher's attention, learning is a competition where students hope to beat their classmates so they can shine. When learning is independent, students learn that they are in it for themselves. In stark contrast, in the classroom that uses Kagan Structures, students interact with each other. They share learning goals. They are on the same side. They hope for the success of their classmates and they help each other learn. Strangers become friends, and bullies become buddies. Discipline problems disappear, replaced by positive social skills and behaviors.

I have now trained teachers in almost 40 countries. In each country I observe classrooms. Worldwide, the most common way teachers are structuring the interaction in their classroom is to ask a question and then call on a student who raises his or her hand. We need to look not at the faces of the students who are raising their hands, anxious to be called upon. We need to look instead at the faces and body language of those who are hiding, hoping not to be called upon. If we want to release the power of active engagement, we need to restructure our classrooms so every student has a voice.

After observing traditional classrooms, I always come away asking myself the same questions:

Why call on one, when we can call on all?

Why engage some, when we can engage everyone?

IN THIS BOOK

WHAT IS A KAGAN STRUCTURE?

Kagan Structures are the core of this series. Kagan Structures are interactive teaching and learning strategies designed to make learning more cooperative and engaging. Structures are a repeatable series of steps that describe how students interact with each other over the curriculum. They may be used with different subject matter and at different grade levels. For example, a primary teacher may use a **RoundRobin** in social studies to have students name community helpers; an elementary teacher may use a **RoundRobin** in science to have students review the steps of a math algorithm; and a secondary teacher may use a **RoundRobin** in language arts to share their written themes of a short story they just read. The steps of the structure are the same across the grade levels and across the curriculum. That's what makes structures so powerful. When you learn one new structure, you are empowered to use it to create engagement in so many different ways.

Kagan Structures were born of the theory and research on cooperative learning. Cooperative learning is one of the most extensively researched educational innovations of all times, and study after study and metaanalysis after metaanalysis has confirmed its superior performance over traditional independent and competitive teaching methods for student learning. Teachers, schools, and districts using Kagan Structures have corroborated the research, reporting giant strides in educational attainment, increases in positive student behaviors, and decreases in discipline problems.

WHY SO MANY STRUCTURES?

There are so many strategies in this book and series because there are so many things we need to accomplish in the classroom. Kagan Structures provide engaging alternatives to traditional teaching. **Centerpiece**, for example, is a way to brainstorm and share ideas in teams. **Fan-N-Pick** is a terrific team structure to review curriculum in a game-like fashion. **RallyCoach** is a pair problem-solving structure—a wonderful alternative to traditional worksheet work. Each structure is good for reaching a different educational objective. Knowing which structure to use and when to use it is part of the art and science of teaching.

Another reason there are so many structures is because students crave novelty. If we do the same thing day in and day out, school becomes boring. It is a monotonous chore where every day looks like the last—different day, same structure. Motivation and learning are intricately intertwined. If students come to class and are engaged with different classmates in different ways, learning isn't stale. Class time is fresh and fun. Teachers who learn and use a variety of structures keep students motivated and excited to see how they will work with their classmates today. If variety is the spice of life, structures are the spice of learning.

HOW ARE STRUCTURES ORGANIZED?

In this book, the main structures are organized alphabetically. However, related structures are nested within a main structure. For example, in the structure **Carousel Feedback**, you will find the related structures **Carousel Discuss** and **Blind Feedback**. Having similar structures nearby shows the relationship of the structure and makes it easy to find and learn comparable structures.

DEDICATION

This book is dedicated to a different vision for education. It is a vision where all students are actively engaged every day. Where teachers have a rich array of structures to promote student interaction over the curriculum. It is a vision in which students are much more motivated to learn because the classroom respects their natural desire to move, interact, and process information. Where students' minds blossom because they understand and retain so much more of what they do and say than what they hear. This book is dedicated to a vision where students feel a sense of belonging in the classroom forged by positive daily interactions where they are known, liked, and respected by their classmates, teammates, and partners.

This book is dedicated to a vision of full student engagement. And this book is dedicated to you—the thoughtful educator who defiantly departs with tradition to embrace a revolutionary new way to teach in order to make this vision a reality for your students.

IN THIS BOOK Continued

HOW ARE STRUCTURES PRESENTED?

Each main structure is presented in the same fashion: The structure has a short synopsis, making it easy to get the big picture at a glance. The synopsis is also helpful when searching for the right structure or for a quick refresher. There is a written description of the structure, painting a picture of what the structure looks like in action. Perhaps most helpful are the step-by-step directions for using the structure.

Please keep in mind that the steps were carefully crafted and each step is there for a reason. Structures are designed to incorporate research-based educational principles and each step has a purpose. If you leave out a step or two, you will diminish the effectiveness of the structure. For example, if you leave out a step, you may be leaving out the element that ensures equal participation for everyone. Or you may be leaving out individual accountability, which is crucial for boosting achievement for all. When we leave out important steps, we water down the structures with deleterious effects on student learning. Using the structures properly maximizes student benefits.

There are also practical tips for using the structure, developed over years of use. Ideas Across the Curriculum offer suggestions for how you might use the structure in mathematics, language arts, social studies, science, and other subjects. These ideas are intended to prime the pump for you to consider how you might use the structure in your own classroom. You know your curriculum best, and we encourage you to brainstorm and jot down ideas for how you can integrate the structure into your own lesson plans.

Some structures also include blackline masters. Some blacklines are templates for you to use as you create your own activities using your own curriculum. Some blacklines are sample activities. These are not intended as activities for you to use with your students, but rather as example activities so you can see how you can design your own blacklines when using the structure. If you are looking for ready-to-use activities, Kagan offers many books across the grade levels and across the curriculum.

Related structures are presented in less detail than the main structures. They offer a description of the structure and brief step-by-step instructions.

Introduction

Structure #1

AGREE-DISAGREE LINE-UPS

Structure #1
AGREE-DISAGREE LINE-UPS

Students line up to agree or disagree with a statement and then discuss their positions.

AGREE-DISAGREE LINE-UPS is a great way to have students clarify and articulate their opinions and beliefs. The teacher makes a statement, taking one side of a controversial issue. For example, "*Capital punishment should be abolished.*" Students think about the statement and decide how strongly they agree or disagree with the issue. Next, they form a line, lining up in proportion to their agreement or disagreement with the statement. The student who most strongly agrees with the statement is on one end of the line. The student who most strongly disagrees is on the other end of the line. The students in between represent the continuum of opinions on the issue. Then the teacher provides a discussion topic. For example, "*Why do you feel the way you do about this issue?*" Students pair up with the student next to them and use Timed Pair Share or RallyRobin to share their thoughts on the issue.

Agree-Disagree Line-Ups is an excellent way to deal with the many controversial topics that arise in the curriculum. Students are given the outlet to voice their own opinions. They take personal interest in and ownership of the content. And importantly, with Folded Line-Ups, they have the opportunity to see and hear the different opinions of their classmates. Agree-Disagree Line-Ups helps students realize that not everything is black and white. There are perspectives and nuances they had never considered.

BENEFITS

Students...

...explore all sides of an issue. (See related structure: Folded Line-Ups, p. 8.)

...take a personal interest in the curriculum.

...develop and articulate their own opinions and beliefs.

...learn to respect opposing beliefs. (See related structure: Folded Line-Ups, p. 8.)

...receive support from peers with similar opinions.

...are energized, out of their seats, and moving.

Step 1: Teacher Makes Statement

The teacher makes a strong statement, taking one side of a controversial issue. For example, "*The United States has the right to declare war on a foreign country if there is a potential or perceived threat to the U.S. even if the threat is not immediate.*"

Step 2: Think and Write Time

Students think about the statement and clarify how strongly they agree or disagree with the statement. "*Think about it: How strongly do you agree or disagree with the statement?*" They can write "Agree" or "Disagree" on a slip of paper, or with more time, they can write a more elaborate response to the statement. "*I disagree; aggression in the name of preemption is not a good foreign policy.*" Students may also select a premade card that represents their position:

- Strongly Agree
- Agree
- No Opinion
- Disagree
- Strongly Disagree

Step 3: Students Line Up

Students form a line in proportion to their agreement or disagreement with the statement. "*Chat with classmates (or show your classmates your response card) to find your place in the line.*"

Step 5: Pairs Interact

Starting on one side of the line, the first two students pair up to face each other. Then the next two, and so on until everyone has a partner. Pairs interact using Timed Pair Share where each partner gets the same amount of time (30 seconds–1 minute) to respond to the question or using RallyRobin where each partner takes a turn stating an idea.

Step 4: Teacher Provides Interaction Topic

Once students have lined up, the teacher provides an interaction topic. For example, "*What does a preemptive strike mean? Is it an acceptable foreign policy?*"

Agree-Disagree Line-Ups

STRUCTURE POWER

Evaluation is an essential thinking skill. As students use their bodies to take a stance, they are engaging evaluative thinking. We know from neuroplasticity research that "neurons that fire together wire together." So Agree-Disagree Line-Ups actually develops the ability of the brain to efficiently evaluate. By having students move to express their evaluation, they also are developing their bodily/kinesthetic intelligence.

TIPS

• **Pairing Up.** To have students pair up to interact, start on one side of the line. Have the first two students pair up, then the next two, and so on. If there is one student left over on the end, have him or her form a triad with the pair in front of or behind him or her. For large lines, it's quicker to have students pair up on both sides. If there is one student without a partner in the middle, he or she can form a triad with the pair in front of or behind him or her.

• **Signs.** To help students line up, make three signs: Agree, Disagree, and Neither. Place the Agree and Disagree signs on the opposite ends of the lines. Place the Neither sign toward the middle.

• **Spectrum Topics.** Use topics that create a continuum of stances. Don't use topics that separate students into distinct groups like eye color, sex, or age.

• **Agree-Disagree Forms.** Provide students with a form so they can mark on the form where they stand on the issue. Next, students write a description of their position on the issue. Students take the form to the lineup and can take turns reading their written opinions during pair interaction time. See sample blacklines provided.

• **Response Cards.** Each student receives a set of response cards. Each card represents a different level of agreement. Students select the card that best represents their level of agreement with the teacher statement. Students show each other their selected card as they line up.

• **Mark the Line.** Prior to lining up, students each draw a line on a piece of paper and label the line with an "A" at one end and a "D" at the other. They then walk alone to mark the line to indicate their stance. This prevents students from simply standing where friends stand and speeds the lineup process.

IDEAS Across the Curriculum

Mathematics

- Problem-solving skills are more important than memorization.
- Students shouldn't have to memorize math facts because we have calculators and computers.
- Students should be allowed to used calculators on math tests.
- Writing about mathematics is not helpful.
- I will need to know a lot of math in my job.
- Math is fun.

Language Arts

- *East of Eden* is Steinbeck's greatest novel.
- Ernest Hemingway is the best author ever.
- Shakespeare's plays will never be outdone.
- Spelling is not important because computers have spell check.
- Having a good vocabulary is an advantage in life.
- I like poetry.
- Students should be required to read at least 30 minutes daily.
- Handwriting shouldn't be taught because printing is easier to read.
- The best way to learn to write is to read.
- The best way to learn to write is to write often.
- I like public speaking.

Social Studies

- The average person today is much smarter than a person 100 years ago.
- Capital punishment should be banned.
- We should abolish all nuclear weapons immediately.
- Students should wear uniforms to school.
- Students should be allowed to use cell phones in school.
- Same-sex partners should be allowed to adopt children.
- Gays should be allowed to openly serve in the military.

- Alcohol should be banned.
- Animals should not be harmed in sports such as bullfights.
- Socialism is superior to capitalism.
- The world population should be controlled by the number of children permitted.
- Voting in elections should be compulsory.
- The government should provide medical coverage to all Americans.
- Corporal punishment is justifiable for criminals.
- Democracy is the best form of government.
- All countries should have the same currency.
- The driving age should be raised to 18.
- Marijuana should be legalized.

Science

- Space exploration is more important than solving world hunger.
- The average life span will exceed 100 in the next 50 years.
- We will never find a cure to cancer.
- In the future, we will grow humans outside the human body.
- Animal testing should be completely banned.
- The common cold will be cured in the next 15 years.
- Nuclear energy is too risky.
- Global warming is a hoax.
- A brain transplant will never happen.
- Extraterrestrial life exists.
- We will eventually have to live in space.
- Humans did not evolve.
- It is more important to protect our oceans than rain forests.

continued

Agree-Disagree Line-Ups

Music

- Classical music is the best music of all time.
- Mozart was the most talented musician ever.
- I would rather be a singer than an instrumentalist.
- The electric guitar sounds better than an acoustic guitar.
- Music classes should be required for all elementary students.
- Computers are the future for musicians.
- Music should be free to download from the Internet.

Physical Education

- Violent sports should be banned.
- Drug testing should be mandatory for all professional athletes.
- Professional athletes should not be allowed to compete in the Olympics.
- There should be no minimum age requirement to compete in the Olympics.
- Physical exercise should be mandatory for every student in public school.
- Individual sports are better than team sports.
- Weight training is superior to aerobic exercise.

Technology

- Technology is making us more antisocial.
- The Mac is superior to the PC.
- The Internet is the best technological breakthrough of all time.
- People will have technology implanted in their bodies soon.
- Cars will be replaced by personal flying crafts in the next 100 years.

VARIATIONS

- **Paraphrase Passport.** In Folded Line-Ups (see page 8), students discuss issues with students of different viewpoints. To validate what the other student is saying, play Paraphrase Passport. Students must paraphrase what their partner said before speaking. Paraphrasing promotes listening skills because students know they must listen if they are to paraphrase.

- **Praise Passport.** Praise Passport is the same as Paraphrase Passport except students must praise the thinking of their partner before speaking. Students feel that their perspective is worthy when it is appreciated. Praise Passport makes students look for virtues in a perspective different from their own. Remind students that they do not have to agree with a point of view to appreciate how well it is stated, the thought that went into it, or the strength of the feelings behind it.

RELATED STRUCTURES

#2 Split-N-Slide Line-Ups

Split and slide the line-up to have students interact with students with different perspectives. For Split-N-Slide Line-Ups, the students in the middle face students on each end. This process creates interaction between students without strong opinions on the issue (middle) and students with strong opinions (ends). Follow these steps to split and slide the lineup.

Step 1 Line Up

Students line up.

Step 2 Split the Line

Split the line in the middle. The students in half the line take three steps forward.

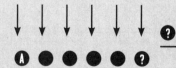

Step 3 Slide the Line

The students in the half of the line that stepped forward now slide down so the two halves now face each other. Students who were in the middle of the lineup now face students on the ends.

Slide

Step 4 Pairs Interact

Students are now in pairs. They shake hands and are ready to interact over teacher interaction topics.

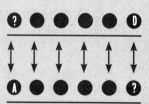

#3 Folded Line-Ups

Fold the lineup to have students interact with students of different or opposite opinions. Once the lineup is folded, the students on opposite ends pair up to interact. Usually, the lineup is folded after students interact in the original lineup. Sharing first with a partner with a similar opinion provides students support for their stance and prepares them with better ideas to share with their new partners. To fold the lineup, have the students at one end of the line walk over to the other end. Students follow the leader so that when they stop, each is across from a new partner. New partners shake hands, the teacher provides an interaction topic, and pairs interact.

Step 1 Line Up

Students line up based on the teacher's prompt.

Step 2 Fold the Line

Students fold the line: Students at one end walk to face students at the other end. Partners shake hands as they pair up.

Step 3 Partners Interact

Students interact with their partners, using:
- Paraphrase Passport
- Timed Pair Share
- RallyRobin

Example: *"Share the reasons you took the stance using Paraphrase Passport."*

Tip

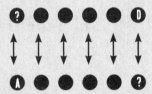

If the line does not divide evenly when folded, the three students in the center form a triad rather than a pair.

#4 Double Folded Line-Ups

After students line up, they do a Folded Line-Ups so that students interact with classmates with different opinions. Then, starting at one end, the first pair walks over to the other side of the line to join the pair at the other end. Each subsequent pair follows the pair that walked, teaming up with the next pair on the opposite side. The result is heterogeneous teams of four.

Here's what it might look like: Strongest Agree and Strongest Disagree students interact after first fold, and then the pair who sees both sides of the issue or who doesn't care strongly about the issue (the middle of the initial lineup) joins them and sit down as a group to discuss the issue. This ensures that all points of view are represented.

Step 1 Line Up

Students line up.

Step 2 Fold the Line

Fold the line in half.

Step 3 Form Teams of Four

Pairs from one side of the line join pairs at the other side to form teams of four.

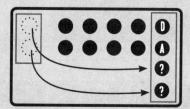

Step 4 Heterogeneous Teams Interact over the Issue

In their new teams of four, teams respond to the teacher's prompts about the issue. RoundRobin is a simple structure to interact in teams.

WHERE DO YOU STAND?
Agree-Disagree Line-Ups

Teacher Instructions. Have each student complete a card before students line up.

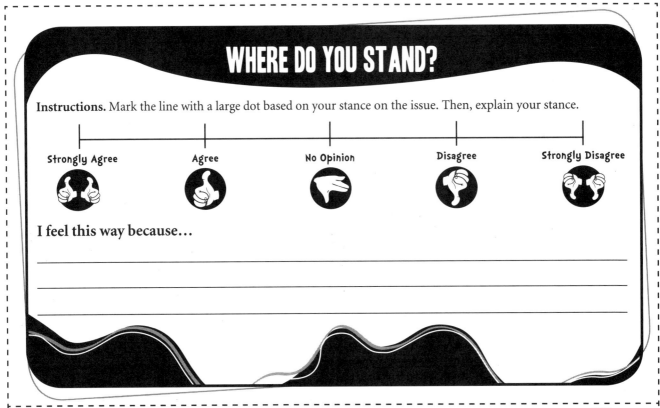

WHERE DO YOU STAND?

Instructions. Mark the line with a large dot based on your stance on the issue. Then, explain your stance.

Strongly Agree   Agree   No Opinion   Disagree   Strongly Disagree

I feel this way because...

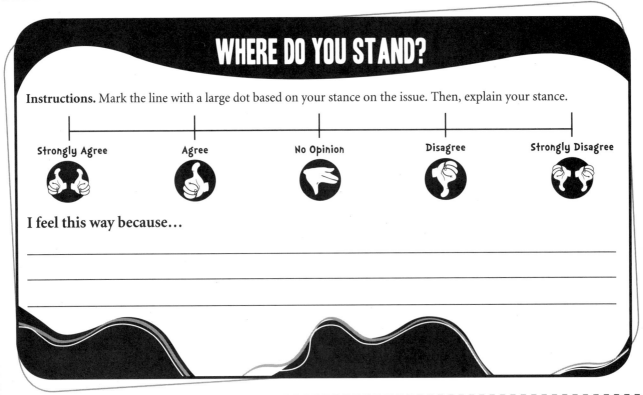

WHERE DO YOU STAND?

Instructions. Mark the line with a large dot based on your stance on the issue. Then, explain your stance.

Strongly Agree   Agree   No Opinion   Disagree   Strongly Disagree

I feel this way because...

DEFEND YOUR POSITION
Agree-Disagree Line-Ups

Teacher Instructions. Have students each complete a card before they line up.

DEFEND YOUR POSITION

Instructions. Circle a number 1–5 that best represents your position on the issue. Defend your position.

Issue

_____

_____

Circle one

1	**2**	**3**	**4**	**5**
Strongly Disagree	Disagree	No Opinion	Agree	Strongly Agree

Defend Your Position

_____

_____

_____

DEFEND YOUR POSITION

Instructions. Circle a number 1–5 that best represents your position on the issue. Defend your position.

Issue

_____

_____

Circle one

1	**2**	**3**	**4**	**5**
Strongly Disagree	Disagree	No Opinion	Agree	Strongly Agree

Defend Your Position

_____

_____

_____

OPINION CARDS
Agree-Disagree Line-Ups

Instructions. Select the card that best represents your opinion on the issue.

OPINION CARDS

Strongly Agree

OPINION CARDS

Agree

OPINION CARDS

No Opinion

OPINION CARDS

Disagree

OPINION CARDS

Strongly Disagree

60 Kagan Structures
Kagan Publishing • 800.933.2667 • KaganOnline.com

AGREEMENT STATEMENTS

Agree-Disagree Line-Ups

Teacher Instructions. Use these sample statements for Agree-Disagree Line-Ups.

- Students should wear uniforms to school.

- Capital punishment should be banned.

- Students should be allowed to use cell phones in school.

- Parents should serve detention with their students.

- Technology will reduce the number of teachers in the future.

- I would live forever if I could.

- Cats are better than dogs.

- Space exploration is more important than solving world hunger.

- Being a pro athlete is a better job than being the president.

- Cake is better than ice cream.

- It is more important to protect our oceans than rain forests.

- It would be better to be rich than famous.

AGREEMENT CARDS
Agree-Disagree Line-Ups

Instructions. Select the card that best represents your agreement with the issue.

AGREEMENT CARDS

YES

AGREEMENT CARDS

MAYBE

AGREEMENT CARDS

NO

ISSUE CARDS
Agree-Disagree Line-Ups

Instructions. Select the card that best represents your opinion or the issue.

AGREEMENT CARDS

FOR

AGREEMENT CARDS

UNCERTAIN

AGREEMENT CARDS

AGAINST

MARK THE LINE
Agree-Disagree Line-Ups

Instructions. Indicate where you stand with a mark on the line.

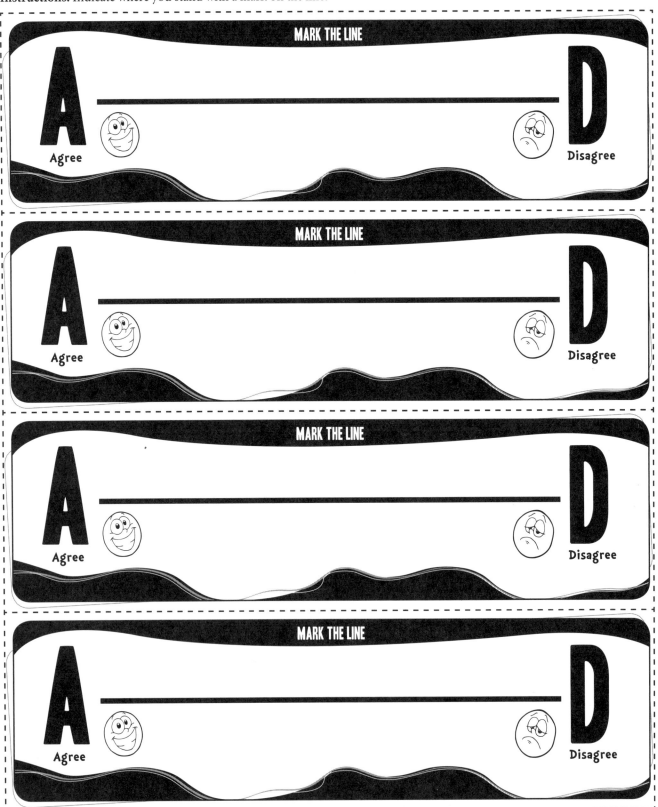

ANSWER-N-EXPLAIN

Structure #5
ANSWER-N-EXPLAIN

Partners each solve a worksheet problem, one explains the answer, and the other coaches and celebrates. They switch roles after each problem.

STEPS Getting Ready
The teacher selects or prepares a worksheet. Students sit in pairs.

Step 1
Students Answer First Problem

Working alone, students answer the first question or solve the first problem.

Step 2
Partner A Explains

Partner A in each pair shares and explains his or her answer with Partner B. For recall questions, students say how they remembered. For procedures and problem solving, they explain the steps they followed.

Step 3
Students Celebrate or Coach

If they agree on the answer, the pair celebrates. If not, they coach, then celebrate.

Step 4 | Students Solve Second Problem

Working alone, students in each pair solve the second problem.

Step 5 | Partner B Explains

Partner B in each pair shares and explains his or her answer with Partner A.

Step 6 | Students Celebrate or Coach

If they agree on the answer, the pair celebrates. If not, they coach, then celebrate.

Step 7 | Repeat

Students repeat the process for each problem on the worksheet, alternating which student shares and explains the answer.

Answer-N-Explain

ANSWER-N-EXPLAIN WORKSHEET

Answer-N-Explain

Instructions. Working solo, solve one problem or question. Pair up to explain your answer. Partners alternate who explains after each problem.

1 **Problem/Question**

Answer/Explain_____
_____
_____

2 **Problem/Question**

Answer/Explain_____
_____
_____

3 **Problem/Question**

Answer/Explain_____
_____
_____

4 **Problem/Question**

Answer/Explain_____
_____
_____

5 **Problem/Question**

Answer/Explain_____
_____
_____

Structure # 6

CAROUSEL FEEDBACK

Structure # 6
CAROUSEL FEEDBACK

Teams rotate from project to project to leave feedback for other teams.

TEAMS CREATE inspired team products. Sometimes teams create works of art such as collages, sculptures, and paintings. Sometimes teams come up with a unique categorization system, mind map, or graphic organizer. Sometimes they create a product such as a poster, brochure, or book. By interacting with each other and the content of the project, students learn a lot about teamwork and the curriculum. But student learning does not end with the completion of the project. The next step is for teams to view other teams' projects to learn from their creativity and to leave feedback so the creators can see how their projects are perceived by others. After projects are completed, there's still a lot to learn. That's where Carousel Feedback comes in.

In Carousel Feedback, each team stands by its completed project. The projects may be on team tables or they may be spread out around the classroom. Teams rotate clockwise to the next project. Teammates examine another team's project and discuss what they like, what they don't like, what its advantages are, and what could be improved. One student writes feedback on a feedback sheet posted by the project. When time's up, all teams rotate to the next project, discuss the project, and leave feedback. The Recorder role is rotated so students take equal turns writing the team's feedback. After teams have viewed and commented on all the projects, they rotate back to their own project. Awaiting them is a feedback form full of comments from other teams. Teams read and discuss the feedback.

Carousel Feedback is a wonderful extension to any team project that results in an observable product. Students benefit from seeing creative solutions to problems, learn to critically examine products, and are celebrated for the fruits of their labor.

BENEFITS

Students...

...practice evaluation skills.

...view and discuss a variety of projects.

...are celebrated for their efforts.

...evaluate the work of others and articulate opinions.

STEPS

Getting Ready
Teams place their team projects around the room. Each project has a feedback form attached.

Step 1
Teams Stand by Projects

Teams stand in front of their own projects.

Step 2
Teams Rotate and Observe

Teams rotate clockwise in the classroom to the next project. They observe the project for 30 seconds without talking.

Step 3
Teams Share and Discuss

Teams do a RoundRobin, with each student sharing his or her reactions to the project. After each teammate has shared, the team has an open-ended discussion about the project and the feedback statement(s) to write.

continued

Carousel Feedback

Step 4
Team Recorder Writes Feedback

For the first project, Student #1 is the Recorder. At the teacher's signal, Student #1 on each team records the team's feedback on a feedback form. The team signals they're done by facing the teacher.

Step 5
Teacher Calls Time

The teacher tells students their time is up. They stop writing and prepare to rotate. "*Time's up. Teams, please rotate together one project clockwise.*"

Step 6
Teams Rotate

The marker or pen is passed to the next student to be the Recorder for the next round of feedback. Students rotate to the next project, read prior feedback, observe for 30 seconds, do a RoundRobin, have a discussion, and leave feedback.

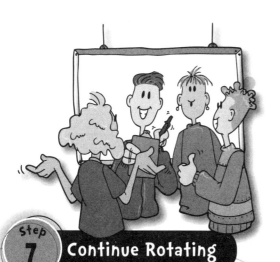

Step 7 · Continue Rotating

Teams continue rotating and providing feedback until each team rotates back to its own project or until the teacher calls time.

Step 8 · Review Feedback

Teams review the feedback they received from the other teams. To equalize participation, teammates take turns reading each comment.

Carousel Feedback

A NOTE ABOUT CAROUSEL

The term carousel comes from a carnival carousel. Kagan Structures with "Carousel" in their title involve teams rotating together as if they were seated on a carnival carousel.

TIPS

• **Space It Out.** Make sure there is enough space between posters or projects so teams have enough room to gather in front of the project.

• **Practice Rotation.** When doing this structure for the first time, have teams do a trial run of rotating clockwise from project to project.

• **Time It.** Give students a time limit for their team discussion and for recording their feedback. Call time for both so all teams are ready to rotate together.

• **Rotate Recorders.** Rotate the Recorder role so every teammate gets the chance to record the team's feedback.

• **Different Colors.** Give each team a different colored marker so it is easy to see which team left which feedback.

• **Sentence Starters.** Posting sentence starters on the board or overhead can help direct student discussion and feedback. Possible sentence starters include:
  • What we like best about your project…
  • Our initial impression was…
  • One idea for improvement is…
  • This reminds us of…

• **Feedback Topics.** Another way to script team feedback is to provide feedback topics for each team to discuss and comment on such as compliment, constructive criticism, or impressions.

• **Criteria Scoring.** Teams can score each other's projects and leave comments on topics such as creativity, organization, and overall impact.

• **Make It Positive.** Teams are instructed that they are to include several positive comments each time they give feedback.

• **Positive Feedback.** As a rule, students must leave at least one positive comment for each constructive criticism they leave. Negative comments are never allowed.

• **Call Time.** Students don't need to rotate to every project. The teacher can call, "*Time!*" to have students return to their projects.

• **Unique Feedback.** Encourage students to write unique feedback so not all feedback is the same or similar.

• **Feedback Stickers.** Younger students can leave feedback by selecting from provided comments such as, "*Cool!*", "*Fantastic!*"

IDEAS Across the Curriculum

Mathematics
- Solutions to a complex trig, geometry, or calculus problem
- Different types of graphs
- Team menu or project

Language Arts
- Teams illustrate posters advertising a favorite book
- Make up new endings to a story
- Mind maps of stories
- Team book/story
- Poem

Social Studies
- Posters of projects
- Models
- Clothing
- Campaign posters
- Maps
- Diagrams

Science
- Classification charts
- Complex new inventions
- Body poster with organs
- Science projects
- Murals
- Cell model
- Animal
- Model
- Diagram
- Table

Music
- Recorded sample of team's music
- Team song or chant
- Poster of an instrument
- CD cover
- Collage on musical genre

Art
- Art pictures
- Team page layout/design

Physical Education
- How-to booklet for playing a sport
- Menu for a healthy meal
- Poster on physical fitness
- Workout video

Technology
- Flyer or poster layout
- Edited video
- Podcast
- Program or software
- Program or software packaging
- Digital song or loop
- Animation

Classbuilding
- Class logo
- Class mascot
- Class rules

Teambuilding
- Team logo
- Team banner
- Team poster
- Team name

Second Language
- Posters of community
- Dialogue
- Skit/play
- Video

Carousel Feedback

RELATED STRUCTURES

#7 Carousel Discuss

This structure works the same as Carousel Feedback, except students do not leave written feedback for other teams. They discuss the project, and then when time is up, rotate to discuss the next project.

Step 1 Teams Stand with Project

Teams stand in front of their assigned projects.

Step 2 Teams Rotate

Teams rotate clockwise to the next project.

Step 3 Teams Observe and Discuss

Teams observe and discuss the project.

Step 4 Teams Rotate and Discuss

Teams rotate and discuss repeatedly until they have reacted to all projects.

Using RoundRobin with Carousel Discuss

For the discussion portion, students can do two rounds of RoundRobin. For the first round, students each take a turn sharing what they like about the project. For the second round, they share an idea for improvement.

#8 Blind Feedback

Encourage unique feedback from each team by hiding the feedback of prior teams. This way, each team is providing its own ideas and not borrowing ideas from previous teams who have left feedback. See Blind Feedback Form.

THE FEEDBACK SANDWICH

One positive approach to feedback that may be used with Carousel Feedback, or anytime students are giving feedback, is the Feedback Sandwich. Students start with a positive comment, provide a constructive criticism, and then end with a positive comment. We are more receptive to feedback when it is "sandwiched" in a positive context.

Beginning   **Middle**   **End**

Positive
Comment #1

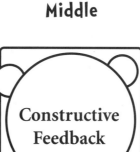

Constructive
Feedback

Positive
Comment #2

CAROUSEL FEEDBACK FORM

Carousel Feedback

Instructions. Fill in your team name, project name, and project description. Post this form next to your team project. One student on each team records his or her team's feedback to your project.

Team Name_____   Project Name_____

Project Description _____

Team 1 Team Name _____
Team Feedback _____
_____
_____
_____
_____

Team 2 Team Name _____
Team Feedback _____
_____
_____
_____
_____

Team 3 Team Name _____
Team Feedback _____
_____
_____
_____
_____

Team 4 Team Name _____
Team Feedback _____
_____
_____
_____
_____

Team 5 Team Name _____
Team Feedback _____
_____
_____
_____
_____

Team 6 Team Name _____
Team Feedback _____
_____
_____
_____
_____

Team 7 Team Name _____
Team Feedback _____
_____
_____
_____
_____

Team 8 Team Name _____
Team Feedback _____
_____
_____
_____
_____

SOURCE: Kagan, S. and Kagan, M. *Kagan Cooperative Learning.* San Clemente, CA: Kagan Publishing.

PROJECT DISCUSSION PROMPTS

Carousel Feedback

Teacher Instructions. Display these discussion prompts for the class to use as they discuss team projects. Alternatively, give each team a copy for them to use as teammates discuss projects.

Our initial impression...

What we liked best...

One idea for improvement...

How complete is the project?

How creative is the project?

PROJECT FEEDBACK
Carousel Feedback

Instructions. Use this form to leave feedback for the creators of the team project.

Criteria Scoring	Score (circle one)
1 Creativity	1 2 3 4 5 6 7 8 9 10
2 Organization	1 2 3 4 5 6 7 8 9 10
3 Completeness	1 2 3 4 5 6 7 8 9 10
4 Presentation	1 2 3 4 5 6 7 8 9 10
5 Overall Impact	1 2 3 4 5 6 7 8 9 10

Feedback _____

_____

_____

_____

_____

_____

_____

60 Kagan Structures
Kagan Publishing • 800.933.2667 • KaganOnline.com

FEEDBACK STICKERS
Carousel Feedback

Instructions. Cut out these stickers. Tape a sticker on the feedback sheet for each project.

FEEDBACK STICKERS

Nice Work!

FEEDBACK STICKERS

Great Job!

FEEDBACK STICKERS

Wow!

FEEDBACK STICKERS

Way to Go!

FEEDBACK STICKERS

Star Work!

FEEDBACK STICKERS

Excellent!

FEEDBACK STICKERS

Fantastic Job!

FEEDBACK STICKERS

Cool!

BLIND FEEDBACK FORM

Carousel Feedback

Instructions. Use this form to provide feedback. Teams leave feedback starting at the bottom of the form, so the form may be folded to hide the feedback.

8 Feedback #8: _____
_____
_____

7 Feedback #7: _____
_____
_____

6 Feedback #6: _____
_____
_____

5 Feedback #5: _____
_____
_____

4 Feedback #4: _____
_____
_____

3 Feedback #3: _____
_____
_____

2 Feedback #2: _____
_____
_____

1 Feedback #1: _____
_____
_____

60 Kagan Structures
Kagan Publishing • 800.933.2667 • KaganOnline.com

CIRCLE-THE-SAGE

CIRCLE-THE-SAGE

Students gather around different "Sages" to learn the content. Students return to their teams to compare notes.

CIRCLE-THE-SAGE allows students with special knowledge or information to become the teachers. The teacher asks a question like, "*Why does snow melt faster when salt is sprinkled on top?*" Everyone who knows the answer becomes a "Sage." Sages stand. All students who don't know the answer, the "Disciples," circle a Sage. Students from the same team each go to different Sages. The Sages enlighten the rest of the class. Students return to their teams and share what they learned from their Sages. Teams make sure everyone knows the answer.

Circle-the-Sage is a great peer tutoring structure, benefiting both the tutor and the tutee. The tutees benefit from receiving instruction from other students in comprehensible terms; often, peers speak the same language. As for the tutors: As teachers, we know the best way to learn and remember something is to teach it. Circle-the-Sage is a great self-esteem booster for Sages who have valuable information to share!

DIFFERENTIATED INSTRUCTION

Selected students may be pre-taught so they are prepared to become Sages on the topic. In this way, otherwise low-achieving students may have the experience of being high-status leaders in the class.

BENEFITS

Students...

...feel a sense of pride when they can teach classmates information.

...receive peer instruction in comprehensible terms.

...are each accountable for sharing what they learn.

...remember what they teach others.

...are members of a community of learners.

STEPS Getting Ready
Each student needs a pen and paper.

Step 1 — Teacher Announces the Topic

The teacher asks a question some students know about and others don't: *"When we are dividing fractions, we multiply by the reciprocal. Who can explain why this is true?"*

Step 2 — Sages Stand

Students who know the answer and feel they can teach the answer to others stand and spread out around the classroom. *"Sages, please stand. Spread out so there is space between each Sage."*

Step 3 — Students Circle Sages

Students who don't know the answer take a pen and paper and circle a Sage. Each teammate circles a different Sage.

Step 4 — Sages Teach

The Sage does his or her best to explain the answer or provide instruction for a specified time. As Sages teach, the other students take careful notes. After the Sage teaches, students are allowed question-and-answer time.

Step 5 — Teammates Compare Notes

Students return to their base teams to compare notes. In turn, each student describes to the team (RoundRobin) what he or she learned from his or her Sage. If students disagree or received different instructions, they see if they can work it out among themselves. If the team can't reach consensus, the teammates raise four hands indicating they have a question for the teacher.

Circle-the-Sage

STRUCTURE POWER

What a self-esteem boost! I become a teacher!
Students experience firsthand that Knowledge =
Status. The Disciples, students who circle the Sage to learn,
exercise their mirror neurons, vicariously practicing being the
Sage. When students return to their teams, often they make a formative discovery: Not all Sages agree.
Discovering that different Sages have given different explanations leads to evaluative thinking and
higher-level synthesis.

TIPS

• **Adjusting the Number of Sages.** The optimal number of Sages is between one fourth and one fifth of the class. Sometimes we can adjust the number of Sages by having many students respond to a question and then having some sit down as we ask more selective questions. For example, we might begin with, *"Stand if you know what mitosis is."* Too many students stand. Then we say, *"Remain standing if you can teach the steps."*

• **Team Questions.** If a team cannot reach consensus on how to solve a problem or there are discrepancies in the information it received from different Sages, the team has a Team Question and all four hands go up. If just one or two teams have a question, the teacher can deal with the teams separately. If more than two teams have a Team Question, teacher instruction to the whole class is in order.

• **Challenging Content.** Circle-the-Sage works best when the concept is tricky and approximately one quarter of the class volunteer as Sages.

• **Select the Sages.** If there are too many Sages or the teacher wants a specific number of Sages, the teacher selects among the volunteers who will be Sages.

• **Knowing and Teaching.** Knowing something and knowing how to share or teach something do not always go hand in hand. If you are focusing on the content rather than teaching skills, be sure to add: *"Stand only if you are sure you can explain (or teach) this concept."*

• **Circle Different Sages.** Teammates should circle different Sages so they have additional or different information when they compare notes.

• **Create Sages.** The teacher may pick a student or some students to receive specialized knowledge or training in advance. The teacher prepares those students to become Sages.

• **Board Sages.** Sometimes Sages will need to write on a board to demonstrate problem solving or make drawings. Sages can use a response board or write on the class board.

• **Topics for Sages.** Sometimes it is helpful to provide Sages guidelines of what to cover as they teach. For example, if they are sharing information about the orchestra, it would be helpful to display a map of the orchestra. Or if Sages are describing microscopes, it would be helpful to display a microscope diagram.

• **Worksheets for Disciples.** Disciples may be given a worksheet with key information about the topic that they need to get from their Sage. Alternatively, the key points could be posted in the classroom. If Disciples are missing information, they may ask the Sage during the question-and-answer time.

IDEAS Across the Curriculum

Mathematics
- Explain how to solve a problem
- Identify solid objects
- Demonstrate how to convert across units
- Identify triangles or polygons
- Explain long division
- Describe the meaning of multiplication
- Compute the volume of a given cylinder
- Create a proof

Language Arts
- Define a word, give examples
- Distinguish between complete and incomplete sentences
- Correct the grammar of a given sentence
- Explain the author's underlying theme
- Define figurative language terms
- Volunteer to demonstrate fluency

Science
- Demonstrate how to build a simple circuit
- Demonstrate a complex lab procedure
- Demonstrate a safety precaution
- Explain a law
- Describe what would happen if…
- Explain why something happened
- Explain a procedure
- Demonstrate how to solve a problem

Music
- Model how to sing a song
- Model how to play a classroom instrument
- Demonstrate the use of music software
- Describe the use of musical elements
- Share knowledge about a musician or band

Art
- Model how to draw something
- Analyze art elements
- Demonstrate a clay sculpting technique
- Describe color theory
- Demonstrate how to clean brushes
- Demonstrate how to create the illusion of depth
- Demonstrate how to mix paints

Physical Education
- Demonstrate a play
- Demonstrate a dance move
- Demonstrate a correct vs. an incorrect technique
- Explain principles of exercise such as progression, overload, and specificity
- Demonstrate a defensive move

Technology
- Model the use of a specific software tool
- Describe how to download a program
- Demonstrate how to organize emails
- Demonstrate how to create a calendar event
- Demonstrate how to use a spreadsheet

Circle-the-Sage

RELATED STRUCTURE

#10 Opinion Sages

Students with an opinion on an issue are chosen to share their opinions. For example, we might say, "*If you have a strong opinion you're willing to share on the problem of illegal immigration, please stand.*" The Opinion Sages spread out throughout the room. Each teammate gathers around a different Opinion Sage to hear his or her opinions. Teammates return to their teams and RoundRobin share what they heard, and then they discuss differences of opinion. Students may be asked to share opinions on cloning, actions of an historical or literacy character, a proposed or existing law, or even how to solve a classroom problem.

Step 1 Teacher Selects Sage
The teacher selects "Sages" to share opinions.

Step 4 Sages Share
Sages share their opinions.

Step 2 Sages Spread Out
Sages spread around the room, standing.

Step 5 Teammates RoundRobin Opinions
Teammates return to their teams to RoundRobin, paraphrasing the opinions they heard.

Step 3 Teammates Gather Around Sage
Teammates from each team gather around a different Sage.

Step 6 Teammates Contrast Ideas
Teammates contrast ideas they heard and discuss their own opinions.

Think-Write-RoundRobin Extension Activity

After students have explored opinions on an issue, they can formulate and share their own opinion. This can be done by having students think about their own opinions, write their own opinions, and then share them with teammates in turn using RoundRobin.

This variation of Circle-the-Sage was conceived of by Bob Henderson.

NOTE-TAKING SHEET
Circle-the-Sage

Instructions. Use this page to take notes on what you learned from your Sage. Compare notes with your teammates when you return to your team.

Topic _____

Sage's Name _____

What I learned...

Additional information teammates learned...

OPINION FORM
Opinion Sages

Instructions. Write your own opinion on the topic. Then take turns sharing your opinions with your team. Record ideas you hear from teammates as they share their opinions.

TOPIC

_____

_____

_____

MY OPINION

_____

_____

_____

_____

_____

_____

_____

OTHER OPINIONS I HEARD

- _____
- _____
- _____
- _____
- _____

CONSENSUS SEEKING

Structure # 11
CONSENSUS SEEKING

Students reach a decision by seeking consensus.

CONSENSUS SEEKING is a process for reaching harmonious group decisions. For example, groups may need to pick a team name. They may need to choose a team topic to research. They may need to select among ideas on how best to present their project. If students can't achieve a "meeting of the minds," problems may arise. A student who does not get his or her way may quietly protest and disengage from the team. When there is no buy-in, students may put forth less effort or refuse to pitch in. Or worse yet, a student may become hostile, feeling rejected by the team. "*That's a stupid idea.*" Since people get emotionally invested in decision making, it is important that the process is diplomatic. Voting creates winners and losers. Consensus Seeking includes rather than excludes.

With Consensus Seeking, the teacher lets everyone know the ground rules: (1) No decision is reached unless all agree; (2) Listen to and seek to understand the point of view of others; (3) Make up your mind only after hearing all opinions, and (4) Don't try to get your way but, rather, try to find something everyone can live with comfortably. The options can be generated by a student brainstorming session, or they can be teacher-provided alternatives. In turn, students RoundRobin discuss their opinions so each student gets the opportunity to express his or her preferences. Finally, students engage in an open discussion striving to reach consensus.

The ability to reach consensus is a wonderful skill that impacts all walks of life. Families choose where to go on vacation. Couples pick a house to create a life together. Companies need to decide where to invest their time and resources. Politicians need to reach consensus on a health care plan. Reaching consensus is often the best decision.

BENEFITS

Students...

...receive the opportunity to share their preferences.

...create a shared goal for teammates by reaching consensus.

...learn to listen for understanding.

...learn leadership skills by including everyone and creating buy-in.

STEPS

Getting Ready
Students generate different possibilities from which to choose or the teacher provides alternatives.

Step **1**

Teacher Describes Ground Rules

The teacher describes the four ground rules:
1. No decision is reached until everyone agrees.
2. Seek to understand your teammates' perspectives.
3. Don't make up your mind until you hear all ideas.
4. Rather than trying to get your way, try to find a solution that works for everyone.

Step **2**

Teammates Share Preferences

In turn, each teammate shares a preference and states why he or she favors the option. For example, "*My preference for our research topic is recycling. If we choose recycling, I found a really good Web site that has a lot of ideas we can incorporate.*" Other teammates listen with an open mind. To equalize participation, students may use Timed RoundRobin.

Step **3**

Students Reach Consensus

After everyone has shared their ideas, the team has an open forum discussion trying to reach consensus. For example, "*It looks like a number of us are leaning toward recycling as the topic. Can we all live with that?*"

Consensus Seeking

STRUCTURE POWER

Through Consensus Seeking, students practice and acquire a life skill. Contrast two groups that are interacting. In one group, individuals are not listening to each other; each is trying to get his or his way. In the other group, individuals are each listening carefully to the others; each is trying to find a solution that will satisfy all interests. Having practiced Consensus Seeking in class, students are more likely to practice it in life. Imagine the kind of society we would have if Consensus Seeking were an interaction style for everyone!

TIPS

• **Can't Reach Consensus.** If students can't reach consensus informally, they may do:
- • Sum-the-Ranks
- • Spend-A-Buck

• **Open Minds.** Young students may need instruction on the difference between getting their way and having an open mind. Emphasize how each of us only has a piece of the pie. Read *Six Blind Mice and an Elephant*.

• **Critiquing Ideas, Not People.** Tell students it is OK to evaluate ideas, but not OK to judge people. For example, it's acceptable for students to say, "*I'm not crazy about that idea because…*" but it is not acceptable to say, "*Your idea is dumb!*" or "*That's stupid!*"

• **Disagreeing Politely.** Teach students gambits for disagreeing politely. Gambits include:
- • "*I respectfully disagree…*"
- • "*I hear where you're coming from. What I feel…*"
- • "*You feel… On the other hand, I feel…*"

IDEAS Across the Curriculum

Mathematics

Teams choose…

- Math-related job to research
- Math project
- Mathematician to research
- Experiment to conduct and analyze

Social Studies

Teams choose…

- Historical figure to research
- Country to report on
- Branch of government to research
- Court case to investigate
- Native American tribe to research
- Explorer to report on
- U.S. President to research
- Best U.S. President

Science

Teams choose…

- Planet to report on
- Invention to make a poster on
- Experiment to conduct
- Body organ to investigate
- Process to report on
- Most influential scientist
- Greatest scientific achievement

Music

Teams choose…

- Song to play
- Musician
- Instrument
- Lead singer
- Body movement
- Team song

Technology

Teams choose…

- Web site name
- Software program to use
- Greatest technological breakthrough

Teambuilding

Teams choose…

- Team name
- Topic to research
- Project title
- Subtopics
- Project roles
- Roles in the team presentation

Consensus Seeking

FOUR RULES FOR REACHING CONSENSUS AS A TEAM

Consensus Seeking

Teacher Instructions. Display these rules as you teach Consensus Seeking and/or while teams reach consensus.

1 No decision is reached until everyone agrees.

2 Seek to understand your teammates' perspectives.

3 Don't make up your mind until you hear all ideas.

4 Rather than trying to get your way, try to find a solution that works for everyone.

CONSENSUS SEEKING WORKSHEET

Consensus Seeking

Instructions. (1) Record each teammate's proposal as it is shared. (2) Reach consensus as a team. (3) Record your team consensus below.

Proposal
1 _____
_____
_____
_____

Proposal
2 _____
_____
_____
_____

Proposal
3 _____
_____
_____
_____

Proposal
4 _____
_____
_____
_____

★ TEAM CONSENSUS ★

_____
_____

SENTENCE STARTERS FOR REACHING CONSENSUS

Consensus Seeking

Teacher Instructions. Display these sentence starters for students as they reach consensus in their teams.

- I respecfully disagree…

- Can we all agree…

- I heard you say…

- Is anyone opposed to…

- I chose _____ because…

- Can we all live with…

60 Kagan Structures
Kagan Publishing • 800.933.2667 • KaganOnline.com

CRYSTALLIZE IT!

Structure # 12
CRYSTALLIZE IT!

First solo, then in pairs, and then in teams, students create summary sentences to crystallize their thinking about a topic.

STEPS

Step 1 Students Write Solo

Students independently write a sentence that summarizes the main point of a lesson or passage.

Step 2 StandUp–HandUp–PairUp

Students stand up, put a hand up, and pair up with a classmate. After pairing, students lower their hands, indicating they have a partner.

Step 3 Partner A Shares, Partner B Responds

Partner A reads his or her sentence to Partner B and then points out why it is a good summary. For example, *"Matter is stuff. I like this statement because it is so short and simple."* Partner B validates Partner A's sentence. *"It's very concise!"*

Step 4 — Partner B Shares, Partner A Responds

Partner B reads his or her sentence to Partner A and then describes why it is a good summary sentence. Partner A validates Partner B's sentence.

Step 5 — Partners Write New Sentence

Together partners write an improved summary sentence. For example, *"Matter is stuff that has mass and occupies volume."*

Step 6 — Pairs Pair

Pairs pair up with another pair to form a team of 4.

continued

Crystallize It!

Step 7 Pair A Shares, Pair B Responds

One student in Pair A reads the pair's summary sentence. His or her partner shares why it is a good summary sentence. Pair B validates Pair A's sentence.

Step 8 Pair B Shares, Pair A Responds

One student in Pair B reads the pair's summary sentence. His or her partner shares why it is a good summary sentence. Pair A validates Pair B's sentence.

Step 9 Teams Write New Sentence

As a team, the students write a new and improved summary sentence.

Step 10 Team Up!

Two teams team up.

Step 11 Team A Shares, Team B Responds

One student in Team A reads the team's summary sentence. A teammate on Team A shares why it is a good summary sentence. Team B validates Team A's sentence.

Management Tip

- Give students a time limit each time they write or share their sentences so everyone finishes at the same time.

Crystallize It!

SUMMARY SENTENCES

Crystallize It!

Instructions. Solo, write a sentence that summarizes the main point of the lesson or passage. Then pair up to write an improved summary. Then form a team to write an improved summary. Finally, team up with another team to share your summaries.

MY SUMMARY (Solo)

IMPROVED SUMARY (Pair)

MORE IMPROVED SUMMARY (Team)

DROP-A-CHIP

Structure # 13
DROP-A-CHIP

Students use up their response mode or gambit chips by "dropping" them on teammates.

STEPS

Getting Ready
Students are provided response mode or gambit chips or make their own.

Step 1
Teacher Announces Time Frame

The teacher announces to the class to "drop" their chips on a teammate or classmate in a given time frame (usually the end of the hour of the day). For example, *"You all have a set of chips. Your job is to drop your chips on your teammates at some point during your social studies project."*

Step 2
Students Drop Chips

Students give their chips to someone when they use them. For example, a student gives her Praiser chip to a teammate as she tells her, *"I really like your idea about making a key for the poster. Smart thinking!"*

Students Use Dropped Chips

After students drop all their own chips, they try to drop the chips that have been dropped on them.

TYPES OF CHIPS

Response Mode Chips

Response Mode Chips describe a type of response to use during an interaction. It is up to students to come up with their own words. Here are some examples:

• Ask a Question
• Ask for Help
• Check for Understanding
• Disagree Politely
• Encourage Participation
• Give Help
• Paraphrase
• Politely Disagree
• Praise a Teammate
• Share an Idea

Gambit Chips

Gambits are specific words, phrases, and sentence starters students use as they interact. Here are some examples:

• Fantastic!
• Wow!
• Another way I see it is…
• Great effort!
• I wonder…
• I agree…

Drop-A-Chip

60 Kagan Structures
Kagan Publishing • 800.933.2667 • KaganOnline.com **59**

PRAISER CHIPS
Drop-A-Chip

Instructions. Use these chips to drop on teammates.

You Rock!	Fantastic!	Great Job!	Thumbs Up!
Awesome Work!	Excellent Effort!	Way to Go!	Magnificent!
Super Duper Job!	Right On!	You're Amazing!	Kudos to You!
Way to Go, Partner!	Your Idea Rocks!	Thanks for Sharing!	Awesome Attitude!

FIND MY RULE

FIND MY RULE

Students practice inductive reasoning as they try to "find the rule" using examples provided by the teacher.

THE TEACHER posts or projects two large boxes and labels them Box 1 and Box 2. Then, the teacher fills in an item in each box. For example, in Box 1 the teacher writes "Book." In Box 2 she writes "Read." The teacher tells the class to think about her rule for placing the items in their respective boxes. Students RallyRobin their ideas with their face partners. The teacher then places another item in each box: "Pencil" in Box 1 and "Write" in Box 2. Students think about the rule and then RallyRobin possible rules with their shoulder partners. When the teacher thinks some of the class may know the answer, the teacher randomly selects a student to test his or her hypothesis by stating an item he or she thinks goes in Box 1 or Box 2. The teacher asks the class if they agree or disagree with thumbs up or down. The teacher then confirms or disconfirms. If the class still doesn't know the rule, the teacher may add more items to the boxes. When the class appears to know the rule, the teacher selects a student to verbalize the rule for the class, *"Box 1 is nouns and Box 2 is verbs."* After a student correctly states the rule, the teacher confirms the rule and then presents the class with new items. The class signals with their fingers which box the next item goes in. The teacher congratulates the class when all items have been correctly sorted.

Find My Rule promotes inductive reasoning: inducing a general rule or principle from specific examples.

BENEFITS

Students...

...develop inductive reasoning.

...practice generating hypotheses.

...verbalize their thinking.

...see content in a graphic organizer.

...develop visual literacy.

...are motivated by a challenging task.

62 **60 Kagan Structures**
Kagan Publishing • 800.933.2667 • KaganOnline.com

Getting Ready

The teacher prepares items to add to each box. The teacher draws two boxes (or other category frames) on the whiteboard, on a transparency, or using PowerPoint.

STEPS

Step 1
Teacher Places First Items

The teacher writes or displays the first items in Box 1 and Box 2. For example, the teacher writes "Snake" in Box 1 and "Cow" in Box 2.

Step 2
Think Time

The teacher asks, "*What is my rule for placing these items in these boxes? Think about it.*"

Step 3
Shoulder Partners RallyRobin

Students pair up with their shoulder partners and take turns sharing possible rules.

Step 4
Teacher Places Next Items

The teacher writes one more item in each box.

continued

Find My Rule

Step 5
Think Time

The teacher states, *"Find my rule,"* and provides Think Time.

Step 6
Face Partners RallyRobin

Students now pair up with their face partners and take turns sharing possible rules.

Step 7
Teacher Places More Items

The teacher places more objects in the category frame, each time having teams discuss possible rules.

Step 8
Student Tests Rule

The teacher randomly calls a student to test the rule; *"Isaac, don't tell me your rule; name an item you think fits in each box."* The selected student stands to share his items. The teacher may ask the class to show thumbs up or thumbs down if they agree or disagree, and then the teacher confirms or disconfirms the answers.

Step 9 — Student Verbalizes Rule

When most students seem to know the rule, the teacher calls on one student to verbalize the rule for the class. *"The animals in Box 1 are reptiles, and the animals in Box 2 are mammals."*

Step 10 — Teacher Confirms Rule

"Do you agree or disagree? Let me see thumbs up or thumbs down. Good, we all agree Sierra has found the rule I was using!"

Step 11 — Class Places More Items

The teacher presents new items one at a time, each time calling for students to hold up fingers indicating the category for the item. *"I have a monkey. Does a monkey belong in Box 1 or Box 2? Hold up one or two fingers."*

Step 12 — Teacher Congratulates the Class

Once all the items are placed, the teacher congratulates the class. *"You have found my rule! Let's do a roller coaster cheer."*

Find My Rule

VARIATIONS

- **Crack My Venn.** Items are placed one at a time in a Venn diagram. Students try to "crack" the titles of both circles. For example, one circle may be cat and the other dog. Place cat characteristics in the cat circle, dog characteristics in the dog circle, and common characteristics in the intersection of the two circles.

- **What's My Line?** Items are placed on a line. Students try to induce the nature of the line. For example, the line can be animal size. On one side would be a mouse, and on the other an elephant. Start with items in the middle and work out to the ends, asking teams to discuss the items at each step.

- **Map My Mind.** The teacher draws a mind map, but instead of writing the central concept first, the teacher leaves it blank. The students' task is to discover what the central concept is as the teacher adds details to the map, stopping for students to interact with each new detail.

- **Discover My Organizer.** Most graphic organizers will work for this inductive reasoning process.

TIPS

Sequence by Difficulty. In preparation for playing Find My Rule with the class, create a list of items. Prioritize the items from more to less difficult. Place the tricky items first so there are many possible rules. Use the giveaway items toward the end so everyone can "find the rule."

Different Sharing Structures. Create novelty by using a different structure each time students interact to share possible rules. Use all three RallyRobin pairings (face partners, shoulder partners, crisscross partners), Pair Share, Think-Pair-Share, RoundRobin, or Think-Write-RoundRobin.

IDEAS Across the Curriculum

Mathematics
- Odd vs. even numbers
- Repeating pattern vs. not
- Divisible by 3 vs. not
- Symmetrical vs. asymmetrical
- Acute vs. obtuse
- Likely vs. unlikely events
- Distance vs. weight
- Concave vs. convex
- Proper vs. improper fractions

Language Arts
- Similes vs. metaphors
- Facts vs. opinions
- Two different story characters
- Subjective vs. objective views
- First person vs. third person
- Spelling rules
- Nouns vs. verbs
- Index vs. table of contents
- Common nouns vs. proper nouns

Social Studies
- Aztecs vs. Mayans
- Obama vs. Bush
- Democracy vs. Socialism
- Democrat vs. Republican
- Constitution vs. Articles of Confederation
- China vs. Japan
- Vietnam vs. Korea
- Dark Ages vs. Renaissance

Science
- Ocean vs. fresh water
- Star vs. planet
- Producer vs. consumer
- Animal cell vs. plant cell
- Mammals vs. nonmammals
- Extinct vs. living animals
- Visible by naked eye vs. not
- Chemical changes vs. physical changes
- Objects that sink vs. float
- Animate vs. inanimate
- Fats vs. proteins
- Aerobic vs. anaerobic exercise

Music
- Classical vs. modern
- Mozart vs. Beethoven
- Violin vs. viola
- Musical career vs. not

Art
- Two dimensional vs. three dimensional
- Orthogonal view vs. perspective view
- Nature vs. not
- Portrait vs. still life
- Warm vs. cool colors
- Radial symmetry vs. not
- Secondary vs. tertiary colors
- Monet vs. Manet
- Impressionist vs. classical

Technology
- PC vs. Mac
- Two different pieces of software
- Software vs. hardware
- Bitmap vs. vector
- CD vs. DVD
- High-tech jobs vs. not
- Things you can do on a computer vs. not
- Digital vs. analog

Find My Rule

SIMILES VS. METAPHORS
Find My Rule

Teacher Instructions. Use the content in these boxes to play Find My Rule on *Similes vs. Metaphors*. Only show one new item from each box at a time.

Box A

- Her anger was as explosive as dynamite.

- Trying to outsmart my dad is like trying to fight a bear.

- The weather was as pleasant as a warm bath.

- The cookies tasted like an old shoe.

- Her smile is as sweet as honey.

- His heart is as big as the sun.

- The moon was like a giant orange in the sky.

- She is as strong as an ox.

- His face was as white as a ghost.

Box B

- He is a sly fox.

- She was a stubborn mule.

- He is a toothpick.

- The quarterback was a lightning bolt.

- My teacher was an angel.

- The aisle in the restaurant was a highway.

- His mind is a sponge.

- Her room is a pigpen.

- She is a firecracker.

60 Kagan Structures
Kagan Publishing • 800.933.2667 • KaganOnline.com

CHINA VS. JAPAN
Find My Rule

Teacher Instructions. Use the content in these boxes to play Find My Rule on *China vs. Japan*. Only show one new item from each box at a time.

Box A	Box B
Total Area: 9,596,961 square kilometers	**Total Area:** 377,972 square kilometers
Climate: Extremely diverse	**Climate:** Extremely diverse
Natural Hazards: Frequent typhoons, floods	**Natural Hazards:** Volcanic eruptions, earthquakes, tsunamis/floods
Population: 1.4 billion (2018 estimate)	**Population:** 127 million (2018 estimate)
Life Expectancy: 76 years	**Life Expectancy:** 84 years
Major Religions: Daoism/Taoism, Buddhism	**Major Religions:** Shintoism, Buddhism
Government Type: Communist	**Government Type:** Parliamentary with constitutional monarchy
Urban Population: 58%	**Urban Population:** 94%
Continent: Asia	**Continent:** Asia
Major Languages: Mandarin, Yue, Xiang Wu, Min Bei, Gan	**Language:** Japanese
Capital: Beijing	**Capital:** Tokyo

MERCURY VS. SATURN

Find My Rule

Teacher Instructions. Use the content in these boxes to play Find My Rule on *Mercury vs. Saturn*. Only show one new item from each box at a time.

Box A	Box B
36 million miles from the sun	890 million miles from the sun
No moons	Many moons (more than 50)
1/3 the size of Earth	9.5 times larger than the Earth
Rocky planet	Giant ball of gas with small, rocky center
One year is 88 Earth-days long	One year is 30 Earth-years long
One day is 59 Earth-days long	One day is 10 Earth-hours long
Cratered surface looks like Earth's moon	Has thousands of rings
Your weight would be .38 times your weight on Earth	Your weight would be 1.08 times your weight on Earth
Small planet	Second-largest planet in the solar system
First planet from the sun	Sixth planet from the sun

PROPER VS. IMPROPER FRACTIONS
Find My Rule

Teacher Instructions. Use the content in these boxes to play Find My Rule on *Proper vs. Improper Fractions*. Only show one new item from each box at a time.

Box A	Box B
1/2	2/1
2/3	3/2
1/4	4/1
3/4	4/3
3/5	5/3
4/5	5/4
3/8	8/3
5/8	8/5
7/8	8/7

FIST TO FIVE

Structure # 15
FIST TO FIVE

Teammates reach consensus by using their fists and fingers to signal their degree of agreement with a proposal.

STEPS

Getting Ready
Teammates prepare proposals to share with the team.

Step 1 — Teacher Explains Symbols

The teacher explains to the class the Fist to Five hand symbols:

- 0 Fingers up (hold up a fist) = No, I cannot live with that decision.
- 1 Finger up = I'm not convinced; let's talk more.
- 2 Fingers up = Not my favorite, but I could go along with it.
- 3 Fingers up = I'm OK with the decision.
- 4 Fingers up = Yes, it's high on my list!
- 5 Fingers up = I'm all for it!

Step 2 — Set Ground Rules

Teams decide up front on the consensus level for an acceptable team decision. Possible levels:

- Simple Vote—most fingers wins
- Low Consensus—all 1s or above
- Medium Consensus—all 2s or above
- High Consensus—all 3s or above

60 Kagan Structures
Kagan Publishing • 800.933.2667 • KaganOnline.com

BENEFITS

Students...

...avoid creating winners and losers created by Yes-No voting. Losers may become disgruntled or unwilling to endorse the decision.

...assess sentiment with a quick poll of the class.

...feel they are part of a team or class decision.

Step 3
Teammates Present Proposals

One or more teammates presents a proposal for the team. He or she attempts to persuade teammates to go for the proposal. For example, if the proposal is for a team name, it may sound like: "*I propose we call ourselves the Shooting Stars. José and Nancy both like Shooting Hoops. Danny and I both want to be actors. Plus, the name sounds cool.*" Alternatively, the teacher, teams, or individual students may make one or more proposals for the entire class. Fist to Five may be used as a quick poll of the class simply to assess opinions, or as a more formal vote on one or more proposals.

Step 4
Teammates Vote

Teammates vote on one or more proposals using hand symbols. They record the outcomes of their votes. After all the proposals have been voted on, the team makes a decision.

Fist to Five

TEAM VOTING SHEET
Fist to Five

Instructions. Record your finger votes for each proposal to make a team decision.

Proposal ① _____

_____

Proposal ② _____

_____

Proposal ③ _____

_____

Proposal ④ _____

_____

Team Decision: _____

Structure # 16

FORMATIONS

Structure #16
FORMATIONS

Classmates excitedly coordinate efforts to sculpt a challenging class formation.

THE TEACHER announces something for the class to form. It can be a very simple formation such as a square. Or it can be very complicated like a working model of the solar system. Classmates make the formation by coordinating their efforts, deciding where each student should stand. More advanced formations include sound and movement. In a model for the solar system, the earth rotates around the sun and the moon rotates around the earth. A train formation is not complete without all class members chanting in unison: *"Chug-a-chug-a-choo-choo!"*

Formations serves as a class energizer at any point in a lesson because students are up and moving. Formations involves whole-body learning and engages spatial memory. Formations has a positive impact on classmate relations and class identity because students all work together to reach the class goal.

DIFFERENTIATED INSTRUCTION

Students may be assigned a buddy so they move together to make the formation.

- A long rope or piece of yarn may be tied at the ends to form a circle. Before the formation is announced, all students hold on to one place on the rope or yarn. They are not to let go as they move, forming the object with the rope or yarn.
- Students may be shown pictures of the formation in advance. For example, instead of saying form a parallelogram, they are shown a picture of a parallelogram.

BENEFITS

Students...

...are actively involved in creating the formation.

...develop a concrete conceptual image of the formation created.

...who are kinesthetic learners receive input in their preferred modality.

...coordinate efforts to succeed.

...accomplish a class goal.

60 Kagan Structures
Kagan Publishing • 800.933.2667 • KaganOnline.com

Step 1
Teacher Announces Formation

The teacher announces the formation for the class to create. The teacher may show the class a picture of the shape or may give the instructions orally. *"Form a capital letter 'A' by standing as a class in the shape of one large capital 'A.'"*

Step 2
Students Create Formation

As a class, students work together to become the formation.

STRUCTURE POWER

Some students are bodily/kinesthetic learners. They don't really "get" Boyle's law until they link arms to form a container with students in the center moving around, representing the motion of molecules. As the container shrinks, they "get it." Heat and pressure increase as volume decreases. Formations is a great tool for early language learners: Even those at the preproduction level participate fully in a Silent Formation (*see Variations*). When the class succeeds in forming a number sentence, complete with the plus and equal signs, there is a palpable feeling of class unity—we did it!

TIPS

• **Use Visuals.** Show students a picture of the shape or item they are to form.

• **Everyone Participates.** Tell the class the formation must involve all students.

• **Increase Difficulty.** Start with easier formations and move to more complex ones. Do a circle before a hexagon.

• **Links.** Give students one large piece of string tied in a circle or many rubber bands linked together. All students hold on to the string or band as they create the formation.

• **Use Props.** Allow teams to use available props in the classroom.

• **Safety Tip.** If students are going to use props, make sure that they are not going to do anything potentially dangerous like stacking chairs or desks.

• **Ensure Movement.** If you are doing multiple formations, ensure students move with each new formation. For example, if students form the word "car" after the word "cat," tell students they must be part of a different letter or change the orientation of the formation so no students can stay in place.

IDEAS Across the Curriculum

Mathematics
- Triangle
- Number 54
- Answer to 3 x 2
- Form AAB pattern
- Number sentence
- Fraction
- Geometric figures
- Numbers (1, 5, 9, 13)
- Operations (+, −, ×, ÷)
- Shapes
- Number sentences (8 + 1 = 9)
- Algebraic equation
- People graphs
- Angles

Language Arts
- Letter of alphabet
- Punctuation mark
- Setting of a story
- Part of speech
- Letters: uppercase and lowercase
- Book
- Abbreviations
- Words
- Scene of a story
- Parts of sentences

Social Studies
- Outline of a state
- Stagecoach
- Flag
- Covered wagon
- Words
- Spell a city
- Land formations
- President's name
- Geographical formations

Science
- Solar system
- Cell
- Atom
- Structure of a molecule
- Food group
- Water cycle
- Tree
- Fish
- Parts of a plant
- Animals
- Simple machine

Classbuilding
- Ice cream cone
- Class name
- Grade level
- School name
- Balloon
- Hat
- Pencil
- Shoe

Formations

VARIATIONS

• **Team Tableau.** The team creates a representational scene by freezing in a particular position, as if in a picture. Tableau or *tableau vivant* (a living picture) comes from drama where a scene is presented on stage by costumed actors who remain silent and motionless.

• **Card Formations.** Give each student a card with something written on it such as a letter. Students make the formation based on the content of their cards. In this case, students could line up where the letter is found on a keyboard.

• **Silent Formations.** Make Formations more challenging and have students participate more equally by announcing a rule: No talking while creating the formation. They must silently signal each other into place.

• **Picture Formations.** Cut a picture into the number of students there are in the class. Each student gets a portion of the picture. The task is for students to position themselves to recreate the picture. If each student is given part of the Eiffel Tower, some students are responsible for the base and others for the tower.

• **Advanced Formations.** Make the formations more elaborate by using objects in the classroom as visual aids. Students may use the P.E. equipment (balls, jump ropes, bats) to form a skeleton or chairs for the seats in the space shuttle. Make the class come alive by having formations that require movement and sound.

RELATED STRUCTURE

#17 Team Formations

Give each team a formation to create. Let the team discuss and plan its formation before forming it. Have the rest of the class try to guess what the formation is.

 Step 1 Teacher Announces Shape

The teacher announces (or displays) an object or shape.

 Step 2 Teammates Discuss

Teammates discuss and plan.

 Step 3 Teammates Form Shape

Teammates work together to form the object or shape.

LISTEN UP!

Structure #18
LISTEN UP!

Students take turns reading to and then quizzing their partners. For right/wrong questions, Partner A coaches and/or praises.

STEPS Getting Ready
Each pair needs reading material.

Step 1 Partner A Reads

Partner A reads the first passage to Partner B. Depending on the students and the content, the first passage can be:
- A paragraph
- A page
- For a specified time

Step 2 Partner A Quizzes

Partner A quizzes Partner B by asking question(s) about what he or she just read. Let students know in advance how many questions to ask their partners (usually 1–3 questions). Also, the type of questions can depend on whether you are working on reading comprehension or thinking skills. If you are working on reading comprehension, the question may sound like, *"Where did Gregory find the ring?"* If you are working on developing thinking skills, the question may sound like, *"What might have happened if Gregory didn't find the ring?"*

Step 3 Partner B Answers

Partner B responds to Partner A's question(s).

Step 4 — Partner A Praises or Coaches

For thinking skills questions, Partner A praises the thought. "*Your idea is clever because…*". For comprehension questions, Partner A praises a correct answer or coaches an incorrect one. "*This is the paragraph where it says where he found the ring. Let's read it again. You got it! By rereading, you found the ring was in the chest.*"

Step 5 — Switch Roles

Partners switch roles, so Partner B now reads and then quizzes Partner A.

Optional

Students may be required to ask specific types of questions using questioning materials such as: Q-Matrix, ThinkTrix, Question Generator, or Idea Spinner. Or students may ask questions provided by the teacher or posted in the classroom. (*Questioning resources available from Kagan Publishing.*)

Listen Up!

QUESTION STARTERS
Listen Up!

Teacher Instructions. Display these prompts for students to use as they quiz each other about what they just read.

- ## Who...?

- ## What...?

- ## Where...?

- ## Why...?

- ## When...?

- ## How...?

LOGIC LINE-UPS

LOGIC LINE-UPS

Teammates use deductive logic to sequence themselves according to clues.

EACH TEAMMATE receives an item card. The item cards are usually thematic. For example, the four items may be modes of transportation: car, train, airplane, and ship. The team stands shoulder to shoulder in a line by its team table, facing the teacher, each student holding his or her item card. The teacher randomly selects one student to be the first Logic Leader. The teacher reads the first clue. For example, "*The car is on an end.*" The Logic Leader tells the team how to resequence itself. If the team disagrees, it states why. Once it reaches consensus, the team moves. The process continues for each new clue. For example the clues for this problem may be:

- **Clue 1:** *The car is on an end.*
- **Clue 2:** *The train is not in the middle.*
- **Clue 3:** *The airplane is next to the train.*
- **Clue 4:** *The ship is on the left of the car.*

With each new clue, the Logic Leader may "test" a new sequence that matches the teacher's clues. When the teacher finishes reading the clues, he or she quickly repeats the clues as the team verifies its sequence and makes adjustments if necessary. After all clues have been read, the teacher selects one team to share its sequence with the class. Teams with the correct sequence celebrate.

Logic Line-Ups is an engaging way for students to hone their thinking skills and communication skills while promoting a positive team tone.

DIFFERENTIATED INSTRUCTION

Similar-ability teams may be formed. The logic problems may then be posted. The problems are sequenced in difficulty order, easiest first. Teams then progress through the problems at their own pace. Higher-ability teams progress through more problems and reach more challenging problems. Lower-ability teams are able to spend more time on each problem.

BENEFITS

Students...

…practice leading others.

…develop spatial vocabulary.

…develop deductive reasoning skills.

…share a team goal.

…enjoy getting up and sequencing themselves.

STEPS

Step 1
Teacher Selects Logic Leader

The teacher randomly selects a Logic Leader for the problem. The Logic Leader stands in front of his or her team. *"Student #1, you are the Logic Leader for this first problem."*

Step 2
Teammates Line Up

In no particular sequence, the other three teammates stand and line up shoulder to shoulder, each holding one item card.

Step 3
Teacher Reads First Clue

The teacher reads the first clue. For example, *"The lion is not in the middle."*

continued

Step 4
Logic Leader Sequences Teammates

The Logic Leader verbalizes how teammates should line up, according to what he or she can deduce from the clue. Teammates are not allowed to talk at this point. *"The lion must be either first or last. Let's try first. Sierra, please stand first in the line."*

Logic Line-Ups

Step 5 — Team Moves

If they agree, teammates move. If they disagree, they discuss until they reach consensus, and then they line up.

Step 6 — Continue Sequencing

The process continues for each new clue until all clues are acted upon.

Step 7 — Teacher Repeats All Clues

The teacher repeats all the clues. The Logic Leader checks the answer and makes any last-minute adjustments in the sequence if necessary.

Step 8 — Answer Revealed

After all clues have been read, the teacher calls one team to share its lineup order. The other teams check for correctness. If a team disagrees, all teammates put a hand up. The teacher calls on a team to see why the teammates disagree.

Step 9 — Teams Celebrate

If the team is correct, it celebrates with a team handshake or cheer. If the lineup is incorrect, the team corrects it and then celebrates.

Step 10 — Rotate and Repeat

The next student becomes the Logic Leader for the next problem. The role of the Logic Leader is rotated for each new problem.

Logic Line-Ups

STRUCTURE POWER

Structure #19

Neuroplasticity research demonstrates that the more we use a part of the brain, the greater the dendritic branching in that part of the brain. If a neural tract is used often enough, it myelinates, greatly speeding the transmission of neural impulses. With practice, we get faster and more accurate at any skill. What does this have to do with Logic Line-Ups? It turns out that brain research demonstrates which parts of the brain are engaged when we solve deductive logic problems. Contrary to the oft wrongly repeated notion that logic is a left-hemisphere function, different types of logic problems are solved by different parts of the brain, and deductive logic is more of a right-hemisphere than a left-hemisphere function. Thus, as students solve deductive reasoning problems, they actually grow new dendrite connections, and, with enough practice, myelinate those neural tracks. Logic-Line-Ups grows brains! What looks like and feels to students like a fun game is really important brain development!

TIPS

• **Left-Right.** If the problem includes direction terms such as "right," "far left," or "to the left of," students line up differently if they are using THEIR left and right or the left and right of the TEACHER. Tell students "right" means the right side in your team. *"Everyone raise your right hand and point that way. That is the right side of your team lineup."*

• **First-Last.** After establishing what "left" and "right" mean, establish where the line starts and ends. Tell students the beginning of the line is on the right side. *"If I say 'first,' it means on the far right side. If I say 'third,' it means third from the right. If I say 'the nurse is standing before the doctor,' it means the nurse is to the right of the doctor. If I say 'the train arrived earlier than the car,' it means the train is to the right of the car."*

• **Random Spinners.** Use a Student Selector Spinner to randomly select which student will be the Logic Leader. Use a Team Selector Spinner to randomly select which team will share its solution.

• **Work Backwards.** When designing the problems, first come up with the desired sequence. Then write the clues that lead to the sequence.

• **Only One Correct Answer.** Clues may lead to more than one correct answer. To reduce confusion, check the clues carefully to verify that there is only one correct answer.

• **Display Clues.** It is helpful to display the clues after they have been read so teams can refer to past clues.

IDEAS Across the Curriculum

Mathematics

Things to line up...

• Numbers
• Decimals
• Fractions
• Shapes
• Addition, subtraction, multiplication, and division signs

Language Arts

Things to line up...

• Letters
• Story characters
• Books
• Parts of speech

Social Studies

Things to line up...

• Historical characters
• Events
• Time periods
• Presidents
• Maps

Science

Things to line up...

• Science lab equipment
• Elements
• Animals
• Food
• Insects

Logic Line-Ups

VARIATIONS

• Answer Back. As an alternative to having one team reveal the answer, the teacher may use Answer Back. The teacher calls out a question, *"Who is on the far left?"* Classmates all respond in unison, *"The lion!"* Teacher: *"Who is next to the lion?"* Classmates: *"The cheetah!"*

• Team-Directed Logic Line-Ups. Each team gets its own set of problems and object cards. Rather than the teacher reading the clues, the Logic Leader reads the clues to teammates. Each team leads itself through the problems at its own pace and checks its work. Teammates rotate Logic Leaders for each new problem.

• Student-Generated Logic Line-Ups. After doing Logic Line-Ups a number of times, older students can be challenged to work in their teams to create their own Logic Line-Ups problems and to lead the class through the steps of the structure. Alternatively, the problems may be traded with another team (Trade-A-Problem) or rotated through the class from team to team (Send-A-Problem).

DINOSAURS
Logic Line-Ups

Instructions. Cut out these cards to use with Dinosaurs Logic Line-Ups problems.

TYRANNOSAURUS
REX

TRICERATOPS

PTERODACTYL

BRONTOSAURUS

SOURCE: Kagan, M. *Logic Line-Ups*. San Clemente, CA: Kagan Publishing.

DINOSAURS
Logic Line-Ups

BRONTOSAURUS
The heaviest of the group weighed about 30 tons. Jurassic and Cretaceous Periods.

TRICERATOPS
Plant-eating dinosaur with a bony crest over the neck, a long horn above each eye, and a short horn on the nose. Cretaceous Period.

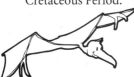

PTERODACTYL
Flying dinosaur of the Mesozoic Era, with wings of skin.

TYRANNOSAURUS REX
Fiercest dinosaur. Flesh-eater. 42 ft. long, 12 tons. Upper Cretaceous Period.

PROBLEM 1
1. The T-Rex is left of the Pterodactyl.
2. The Triceratops is not before the T-Rex.
3. T-Rex and the Brontosaurus are on an end.
4. The Pterodactyl is before the Triceratops.

PROBLEM 2
1. The winged reptile is on an end.
2. The horned dinosaur is on the other end.
3. The heaviest dinosaur is third.
4. The fiercest dinosaur is on the right of the flying reptile.

PROBLEM 3
1. The Brontosaurus is not beside the Pterodactyl.
2. The T-Rex is either first or last.
3. There are two dinosaurs between the T-Rex and the Pterodactyl.
4. The Triceratops is on the left of the Pterodactyl.

PROBLEM 4
1. There are at least two dinosaurs before the T-Rex.
2. The Brontosaurus is not in the middle.
3. The Triceratops is beside the Brontosaurus.
4. The T-Rex is before the Pterodactyl.

PROBLEM 5
1. The Triceratops is not first or third.
2. The Brontosaurus is not third or fourth.
3. The Pterodactyl has three dinosaurs after it.
4. The T-Rex is first or third.

PROBLEM 6
1. The Pterodactyl and the T-Rex are in the middle.
2. The Triceratops is not first and is beside the Pterodactyl.

ANSWERS
1. T-Rex, Pterodactyl, Triceratops, Brontosaurus
2. Pterodactyl, T-Rex, Brontosaurus, Triceratops
3. T-Rex, Brontosaurus, Triceratops, Pterodactyl
4. Brontosaurus, Triceratops, T-Rex, Pterodactyl
5. Pterodactyl, Brontosaurus, T-Rex, Triceratops
6. Brontosaurus, T-Rex, Pterodactyl, Triceratops

SOURCE: Kagan, M. *Logic Line-Ups*. San Clemente, CA: Kagan Publishing.

FUN WHEELS
Logic Line-Ups

Instructions. Cut out these cards to use with Fun Wheels Logic Line-Ups problems.

Bicycle

Skateboard

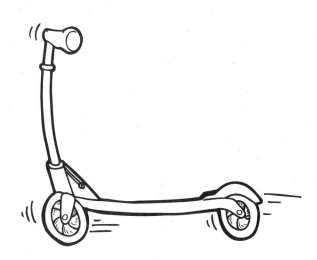

Scooter

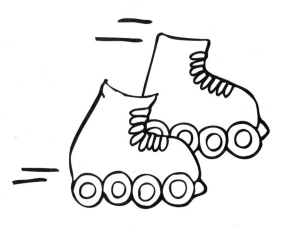

Inline Skates

FUN WHEELS
Logic Line-Ups

Problem 1

1. The scooter is third or fourth.
2. The bike is first or second.
3. The skateboard is not third or fourth.
4. The bike comes before the skateboard.
5. The scooter is not last.

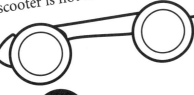

Problem 2

1. The bike is not on either end.
2. The skates are not on either end.
3. The scooter is third or fourth.
4. The skates are not next to the skateboard.

Problem 3

1. The bike is next to the skates.
2. The skateboard is next to the skates.
3. Nothing comes after the skateboard.

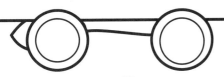

Problem 4

1. The bike is not last.
2. The skates are next to the bike.
3. The bike is not in the middle.
4. The scooter is not last.

Problem 5

1. Only the bike is next to the skates.
2. The skateboard is not on an end.
3. Only the skateboard is next to the scooter.
4. The skateboard is after the bike.

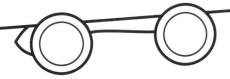

Problem 6

1. The skateboard and skates are before the bike.
2. Either the skates or the bike are first.
3. The bike is not next to the skates.
4. The bike is not on an end.

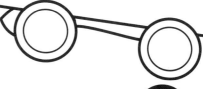

Answers

1. Bike, Skateboard, Scooter, Skates
2. Skateboard, Bike, Skates, Scooter
3. Scooter, Bike, Skates, Skateboard
4. Bike, Skates, Scooter, Skateboard
5. Skates, Bike, Skateboard, Scooter
6. Skates, Skateboard, Bike, Scooter

LOOK-WRITE-DISCUSS

Structure # 20
LOOK-WRITE-DISCUSS

Students write about and discuss an object after it has been removed from view.

STEPS

Getting Ready
The teacher selects an object or visual (or an object for each team). Students each need a pen and paper.

Step 1 — Students Look

Students take a sustained, silent look at an object. The object can be anything visual. It can be an animal for science. It can be a graph for math. It can be a map or picture for social studies. It can be a flower for descriptive writing in language arts. The object can be a different object for each team (team led), or it can be one object displayed in front of the class or on the board for the entire class to see (teacher led). Students are given a time limit to observe the object. *"Take a good, hard look at this diagram. In 1 minute I will hide it, and you will have to write everything you can remember about the diagram. No talking. No writing. Just carefully observe for 1 minute. Begin!"*

Step 2 — Hide Object

The object is placed out of sight. If it is displayed digitally, the projector or whiteboard is turned off. If it is a tangible item, it is placed under the desk so no one can see it.

Step 3 — Students Write

Students independently write about the characteristics of the object for a specified time. *"No talking. Everyone, please write your own description of the diagram. Pretend you are describing it to a friend who is blind. You have 3 minutes. When time is up, you will each share your description, so do the best you can to describe it."*

Step 4   Pairs Read and Discuss

Students pair up. Partner A reads his or her description to Partner B. Then Partner B reads his or her description. Then they have an open-ended discussion about the object.

Step 5   Students Evaluate Writing

The object is placed in view again. In their same pairs, students evaluate the quality of their writing. *"Look again at the diagram. How well did you describe it? What did you remember correctly? What is different from what you recalled? What did you leave out?"*

Look-Write-Discuss

PHOTOSYNTHESIS
Look-Write-Discuss

Instructions. Study this illustration of photosynthesis for 1 minute. Then place it out of sight. Write what you understand and recall. Then pair up to discuss with a partner. When done, bring the image back and evaluate how well you did.

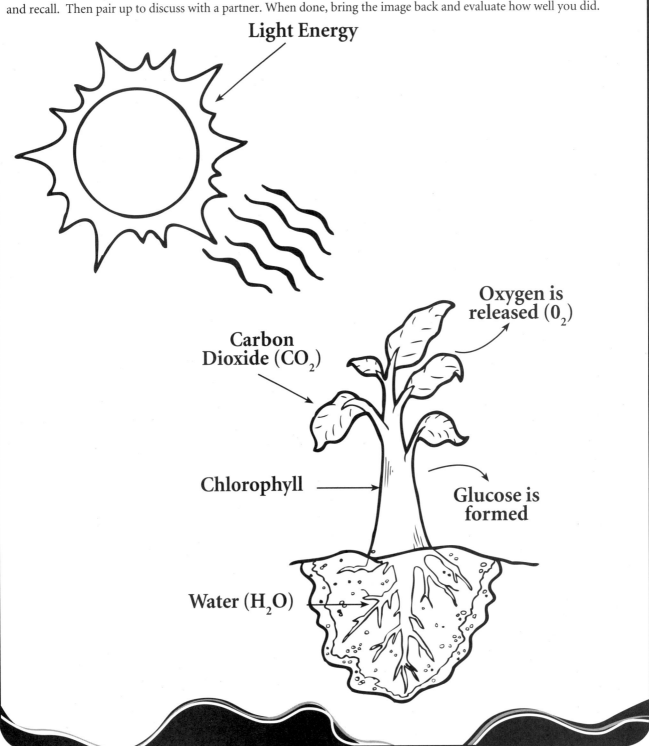

Light Energy

Oxygen is released (O_2)

Carbon Dioxide (CO_2)

Chlorophyll

Glucose is formed

Water (H_2O)

 60 Kagan Structures
Kagan Publishing • 800.933.2667 • KaganOnline.com

Look-Write-Discuss

Instructions. Take a good look at this chart for 30 seconds, and then place it out of sight. Write what you recall and understand about the chart. Then pair up to discuss with a partner when done. Take another look at the chart and evaluate how well you did.

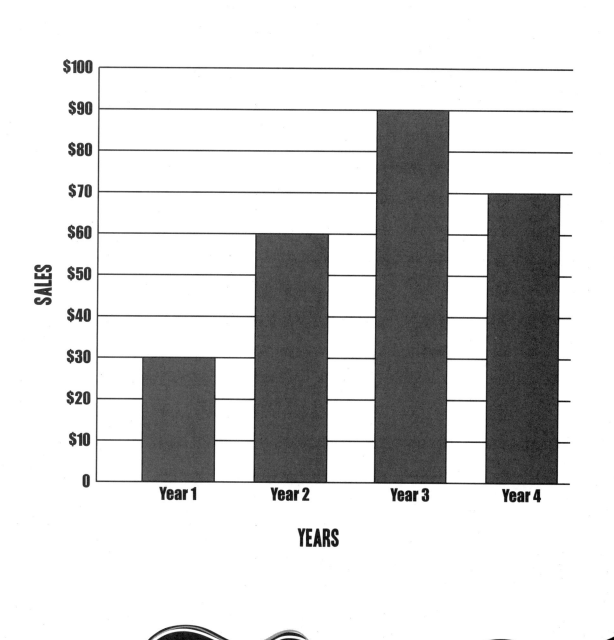

VOLCANO MAIN FEATURES
Look-Write-Discuss

Instructions. Look at this illustration of the cross section of an erupting volcano. Then place it out of sight. Write what you recall. Then pair up to discuss it with a partner. When done, bring back the image and evaluate how well you did.

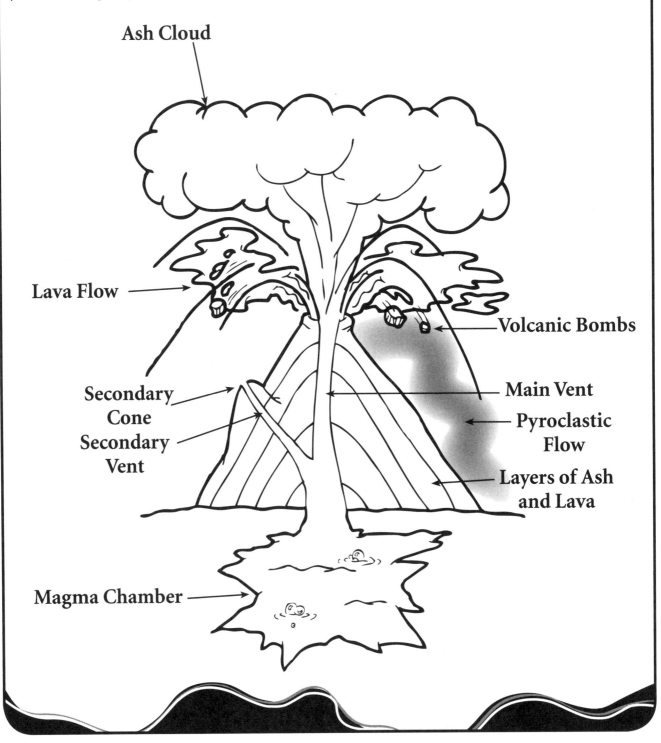

Ash Cloud

Lava Flow

Volcanic Bombs

Secondary Cone Secondary Vent

Main Vent

Pyroclastic Flow

Layers of Ash and Lava

Magma Chamber

Structure # 21

MATCH MINE

MATCH MINE

Partners on opposite sides of a barrier must communicate with precision in order for one to match the other's arrangement of game pieces on a game board.

STUDENTS PAIR UP. Each partner receives an identical game board and game pieces. The game board and game pieces can be based on any subject. For learning coordinates in math, the game board may be a numbered grid; the game pieces are geometric shapes. The pair sets up a file folder barrier between them so they can't see each other's game boards. One partner is the Sender and the other is the Receiver. The Sender arranges the geometric shapes on his or her sheet of graph paper. Then the Sender describes his or her arrangement of game pieces on the game board, and the Receiver attempts to match the Sender's arrangement exactly. "*The top right corner of my square is right in the middle of the grid, on coordinate (8, 8).*" When the pair thinks that they have correctly matched all the game pieces on the game board, the Sender and Receiver compare their arrangements to see how well they did. If the game pieces are arranged identically, the pair celebrates their success. If the game pieces don't match, they congratulate their efforts and then discuss how they could have communicated better to make the match.

Match Mine develops visual thinking, perspective taking, and communication skills. It also creates very strong interdependence because neither partner can succeed without the help of the other.

DIFFERENTIATED INSTRUCTION

Ability groups can play at the appropriate level:

Easiest: Students play side-by-side so they can see each other's boards.

Easy: Items are placed on a line.

Easy: Students play doubles, two on each side. Coaching is allowed.

Not As Easy: Items are placed in two dimensions, on a board.

Difficult: No questions are allowed.

Difficult: Students pass notes up and back, with no talking. (See *Build-What-I-Write*, p. 111.)

Very Difficult: Items are placed in three dimensions.

BENEFITS

Students...

...develop perspective taking as they must imagine themselves in the role of another.

...develop strong verbal communication skills; they must describe what another can't see.

...develop analytic skills as students carefully examine their own arrangements.

...reach a shared goal with their partners through cooperation and coordinating efforts.

...develop vocabulary based on the content of the game board and game pieces.

...develop spatial vocabulary (right, left, next, top, above ...).

STEPS

Getting Ready
Partners, one the Sender and the other the Receiver, sit on opposite sides of a barrier with identical game boards and game pieces.

Step 1 — Sender Creates Arrangement

The Sender arranges his or her game pieces on his or her game board while the Receiver waits quietly.

Step 2 — Sender Directs Receiver

The Sender gives the Receiver directions to match the Sender's arrangement of game pieces on the game board. The Receiver follows the Sender's directions. *"I created a robot using my shapes. Let's start with the head of the robot. Find your biggest blue circle. Now place the top of the circle 1 inch down from the top of the middle of your game board. Next, find the medium red rectangle…"* .

Step 3 — Partners Check

When finished, partners carefully set game boards side by side to check for accuracy. *"OK, it sounds like we have a match. Let's check."*

continued

Match Mine

Step 4 Praise and Plan

The Receiver praises the Sender for his or her instructions, and they develop improvement strategies. *"Great job describing your robot. It was really helpful when you told me the size and color of the shape to use."*

Step 5 Switch Roles

The Receiver now becomes the Sender, and the Sender becomes the Receiver. The pair plays again.

STRUCTURE POWER

From the perspective of the students, they get to play a fun game! From the perspective of the teacher, students are acquiring critical communication skills: unambiguous language, checking for understanding, asking for clarification, and getting supportive comments. But there is more. Students acquire vocabulary in the content area, as well as teamwork skills. The more often we place students in situations in which they must cooperate to succeed, the more we are helping them hone their ability to work with others. They become more cooperative. In the interdependent workplace of today, teamwork skills—the ability to coordinate efforts with others—increasingly rise to the top as predictors of success.

TIPS

• **Communication Skills.** Have students work on their communication skills. Model for students two core communication competencies: (1) asking for clarification and (2) checking for understanding. Play Match Mine as a model for the class and exaggerate any communication errors that can happen if students fail to ask for clarification and/or check for understanding. After modeling, have students reflect on the importance of these two skills. After they play Match Mine, have students process how well they have used these two core communication competencies.

• **Face Partners.** When playing in base teams, use face partners instead of shoulder partners so partners cannot see each other's board and pieces.

• **File Folder Barriers.** File folder barriers are very simple to build. Give each pair two file folders and one paper clip. The pair clips the file folders together at the top with a paper clip, spreads the base, and presto! The partners have a stand-alone buddy barrier.

• **More Barriers.** Other possible barriers include an open textbook, a three ring binder, or a cardstock barrier.

• **Back to Back.** Instead of using buddy barriers, have pairs work back to back on the floor.

• **Storing Barriers.** When done playing Match Mine, have students fold down their barriers and store them for next time. Use sandwich baggies to store game pieces. The baggies and game pieces may be secured with the paper clip.

• **Sponge Activity.** Pairs finish at different rates. Have them switch roles of Senders and Receivers and play again.

Match Mine

IDEAS Across the Curriculum

Mathematics

- Fractions
- Sequencing–1st, 2nd, 3rd, 4th
- Inside vs. outside
- Small, medium, large
- In front, behind, on top
- Shapes
- Tangram

Language Arts

- Building a town
- Food in a refrigerator

Social Studies

- Directions NESW
- Build a world with landforms

Science

- Cell structure
- Parts of a flower
- Endangered species
- Rocks and minerals
- Bones
- Organs

Art

- Tools and supplies

VARIATIONS

• **Team Match Mine.** Match Mine may also be played with two students on each side of the barrier. With pairs on each side, the two Senders take turns (RallyRobin) describing the layout. The two Receivers take turns arranging the pieces (RallyTable).

• **Match Quest.** Two students are on opposite sides of a barrier. They have sheets with the same items on them, but the items are not arranged in the same way. For example, the items may be four very similar clowns, yet each differing slightly. Partner A selects and circles one of the clowns. Then Partner B must ask yes/no questions to discover which clown Partner A selected. *"Does your clown have a hat?"*

• **Build As You Go.** Rather than the Sender building the layout in advance and describing the completed arrangement to the Receiver, the Sender describes his or her arrangement as he or she builds it.

• **Build-What-I-Write.** Have the Senders arrange game pieces, make a design, or create a project. Then, instead of verbally describing it to the Receivers, the Senders describe it in writing as well as they can. The Senders give the Receivers a written description and see how well the Receivers can build what the Senders have written.

Match Mine

HUMAN BODY (Game Board)
Match Mine

Instructions. Use numbers to label each body part.

60 Kagan Structures
Kagan Publishing • 800.933.2667 • KaganOnline.com

SOURCE: Kagan, M. *Match Mine Language Builder*. San Clemente, CA: Kagan Publishing.

HUMAN BODY
Match Mine

Instructions. Cut out each number. Use the numbers to label the body parts on the Human Body game board.

Game Pieces—Partner A

1	2	3	4	5	6
7	8	9	10	11	12
13	14	15	16	17	18
19	20	21	22	23	24

Game Pieces—Partner B

1	2	3	4	5	6
7	8	9	10	11	12
13	14	15	16	17	18
19	20	21	22	23	24

SOURCE: Kagan, M. *Match Mine Language Builder.* San Clemente, CA: Kagan Publishing.

LINE SLOPE (Game Board)
Match Mine

60 Kagan Structures
Kagan Publishing • 800.933.2667 • KaganOnline.com

Instructions. Cut out each Line Slope piece. Arrange line slope pieces on the Line Slope game board to play Match Mine.

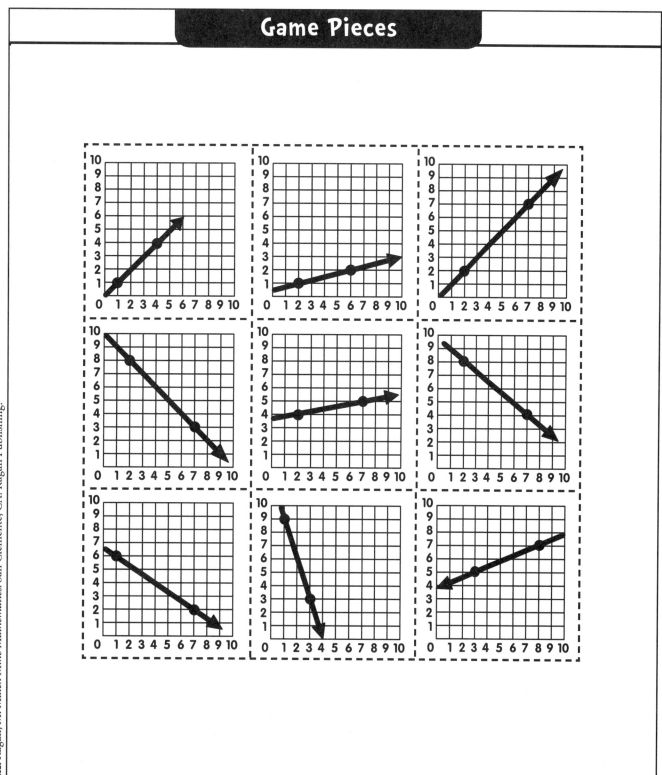

MIX-N-MATCH

Structure # 22
MIX-N-MATCH

Students mix, repeatedly quizzing new partners and trading cards. Afterwards, they rush to find a partner with the card that matches theirs.

STEPS

Getting Ready
The teacher provides or students create pairs of matching cards. One card may have a clockface and the other the time.

Step 2
Partner A Asks Question

In the pair, Partner A asks Partner B a question from his or her card. For example, *"What time does my clock read?"*

Step 1
Students Mix and Pair

With a card in one hand and the other hand raised, each student mixes around the room, looking for a partner with a raised hand. When they pair up, they give each other a high five. *"Pair up with another student with a raised hand. Give each other a high five and lower your hands."*

Step 3
Partner B Answers

Partner B answers Partner A's question. *"It's 10:40."*

Step 4

Partner A Praises or Coaches

If Partner B answers correctly, Partner A praises him or her. *"Right! You are great at reading time."* If Partner B answers incorrectly, Partner A provides the correct answer and coaches or tutors Partner B. *"Close. It's 10:40. You can tell it's ten because the little hand is not all the way to eleven yet."*

Step 5

Switch Roles

Partners switch roles. Partner B now asks the question and offers praise or coaching. Questions will vary depending on the cards. *"Where would the clock hands point for 10:40?"*

continued

Mix-N-Match

Step 6 — Partners Trade Cards

Before departing and looking for new partners, partners thank each other and trade cards. This way, students practice twice as many cards.

Step 7 — Continue Quizzing and Trading

Partners split up and continue quizzing and getting quizzed by new partners. When done, they trade cards again and find a new partner.

Step 8 — Teacher Calls, "Freeze"

After a sufficient time of quizzing and trading cards, the teacher calls, "Freeze." Students freeze, hide their cards, and think of their match.

Step 9 Find Match

The teacher calls, *"Match."* Students search for a classmate with the matching card. When they find each other, they move to the outside of the classroom and stand shoulder to shoulder. This way, students still searching for a match can find each other more easily.

Step 10 Teacher Checks Answer

The teacher selects a pair to begin. The pair shares their answer by stating what they have on their own cards. For example, one partner says, *"I have 10:40,"* and the other partner says, *"My clockface shows 10:40."* Alternatively, the teacher has students hold up their cards and does a quick visual answer check.

Mix-N-Match

BODY PARTS (Sample Cards)
Mix-N-Match

Teacher Instructions. These are sample cards. To play, each student receives a unique card. Students match the body part to its correct definition.

Arteries

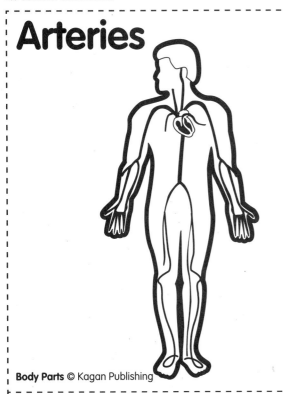

Body Parts © Kagan Publishing

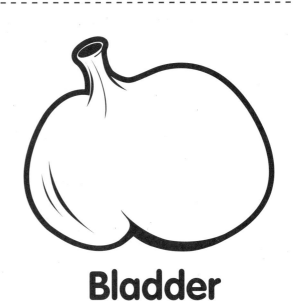

Bladder

Body Parts © Kagan Publishing

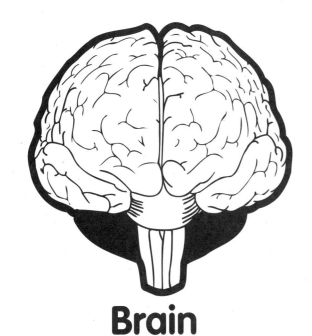

Brain

Body Parts © Kagan Publishing

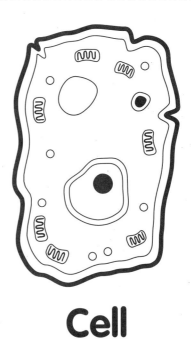

Cell

Body Parts © Kagan Publishing

SOURCE: Kagan, M. *Mix-N-Match: Science.* San Clemente, CA: Kagan Publishing.

BODY PARTS (Sample Cards)
Mix-N-Match

Teacher Instructions. These are sample cards. To play, each student receives a unique card. Students match the body part to its correct definition.

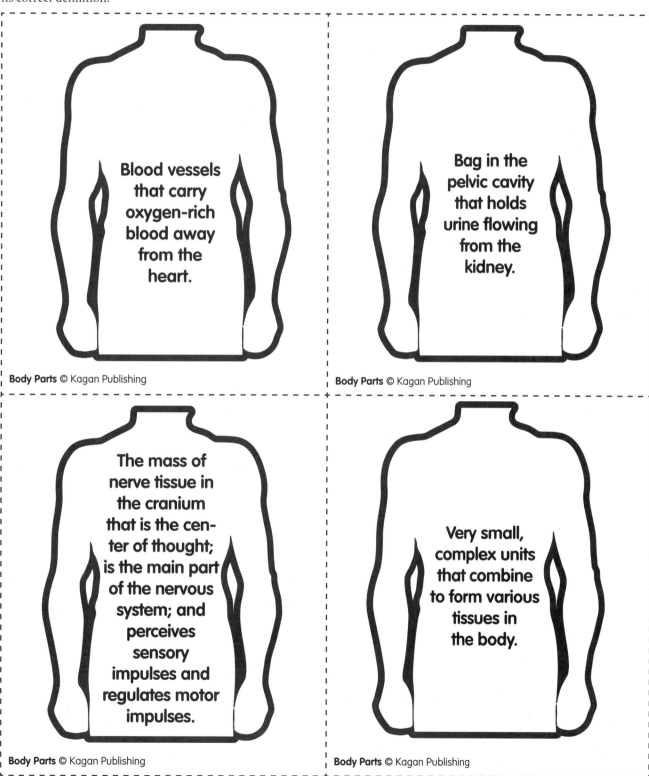

Blood vessels that carry oxygen-rich blood away from the heart.

Body Parts © Kagan Publishing

Bag in the pelvic cavity that holds urine flowing from the kidney.

Body Parts © Kagan Publishing

The mass of nerve tissue in the cranium that is the center of thought; is the main part of the nervous system; and perceives sensory impulses and regulates motor impulses.

Body Parts © Kagan Publishing

Very small, complex units that combine to form various tissues in the body.

Body Parts © Kagan Publishing

SOURCE: Kagan, M. *Mix-N-Match: Science.* San Clemente, CA: Kagan Publishing.

PREFIXES (Sample Cards)
Mix-N-Match

Teacher Instructions. These are sample cards. To play, each student receives a unique card. Students match the prefix to its correct meaning.

intra-

Prefixes © Kagan Publishing

mal-

Prefixes © Kagan Publishing

mega-

Prefixes © Kagan Publishing

multi-

Prefixes © Kagan Publishing

SOURCE: Kagan, M. *Mix-N-Match: Language Arts.* San Clemente, CA: Kagan Publishing.

PREFIXES (Sample Cards)
Mix-N-Match

Teacher Instructions. These are sample cards. To play, each student receives a unique card. Students match the prefix to its correct meaning.

within

Prefixes © Kagan Publishing

bad

Prefixes © Kagan Publishing

large

Prefixes © Kagan Publishing

many, much

Prefixes © Kagan Publishing

SOURCE: Kagan, M. *Mix-N-Match: Language Arts.* San Clemente, CA: Kagan Publishing.

READING TIME (Sample Cards)
Mix-N-Match

Teacher Instructions. These are sample cards. Students match the digital clock time to the analog clock.

Reading Time © Kagan Publishing

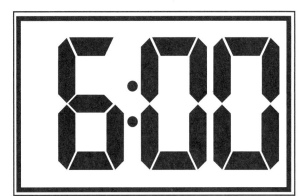

Reading Time © Kagan Publishing

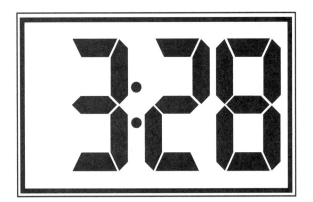

Reading Time © Kagan Publishing

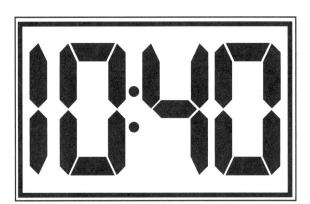

Reading Time © Kagan Publishing

SOURCE: Kagan, M. *Mix-N-Match: Mathematics.* San Clemente, CA: Kagan Publishing.

Teacher Instructions. These are sample cards. Students match the digital clock time to the analog clock.

Reading Time © Kagan Publishing

Reading Time © Kagan Publishing

Reading Time © Kagan Publishing

Reading Time © Kagan Publishing

SOURCE: Kagan, M. *Mix-N-Match: Mathematics.* San Clemente, CA: Kagan Publishing.

LANDFORMS (Sample Cards)
Mix-N-Match

Teacher Instructions. These are sample cards. Students match the landform to its correct definition.

Bay

Landforms© Kagan Publishing

Canyon

Landforms© Kagan Publishing

Delta

Landforms© Kagan Publishing

Desert

Landforms© Kagan Publishing

SOURCE: Kagan, M. *Mix-N-Match: Social Studies.* San Clemente, CA: Kagan Publishing.

LANDFORMS (Sample Cards)
Mix-N-Match

Teacher Instructions. These are sample cards. Students match the landform to its correct definition.

Area of an ocean, sea, or lake that extends into the land. Usually smaller than a gulf.

Landforms© Kagan Publishing

A deep, narrow valley with steep sides and often with a river or stream on its floor.

Landforms© Kagan Publishing

Small islands of sediment that divide a river into smaller parts at its mouth.

Landforms© Kagan Publishing

Dry and often hot areas that receive very little precipitation.

Landforms© Kagan Publishing

SOURCE: Kagan, M. *Mix-N-Match: Social Studies.* San Clemente, CA: Kagan Publishing.

OBSERVE-WRITE-ROUNDROBIN

Structure # 23

OBSERVE-WRITE-ROUNDROBIN

Students receive immediate feedback on their observation and writing skills.

STEPS

Getting Ready

The teacher prepares objects for students to observe and describe. The teacher may also instruct students about observation skills and descriptive writing skills.

Step 1 — Students Observe and Write

An item is placed in view of students. The item can be a picture for history, a book cover for language arts, a map for geography, or a process or cycle for science. It can be displayed in front of the class or on the board, or each team or student can have a copy. While observing, students work alone and describe the item in writing.

Step 2 — Hide Object

The object is placed out of sight. If it is displayed digitally, the projector or whiteboard is turned off. If it is a tangible item, it is covered up or placed under the desk so no one may see it.

DIFFERENTIATED INSTRUCTION

Students, in consultation with the teacher, can choose developmentally appropriate objects to draw. For those students who need it, a Scribe can help record their observations.

Step 3 Teammates Share Writing

Students RoundRobin read their written descriptions in their teams.

Step 4 Objects Returned

After each teammate has read his or her description, they signal they are done. When everyone is ready, the object is returned to view.

continued

Step 5 — Students RoundRobin New Ideas

Students look again at the item and take turns stating new words, phrases, or sentences about the item that they did not have in their own writing. This pushes students to look at the item from a new or more detailed perspective. As teammates suggest new ideas, students may make notes.

Step 6 — Students Improve Writing

Students improve their writing by adding ideas they heard from teammates and/or elaborating on their notes from the second RoundRobin.

Look-Write-Discuss vs. Observe-Write-RoundRobin

Observe-Write-RoundRobin develops observation and writing skills. In addition to observation and writing skills, because the object is out of sight during the writing phase, Look-Write-Discuss fosters an additional skill: memory.

#24 Observe-Draw-RoundRobin

Observe-Draw-RoundRobin is the same as Observe-Write-RoundRobin except, instead of writing about the item, students draw the item.

Getting Ready
The teacher prepares objects for students to draw. It can be one object displayed for the class or one object for each team.

Step 1 Students Observe and Draw

An item is placed in view of students. The item must be something students may draw. For example, it could be a graph, a picture, an object, a visual organizer, or a map. While observing, students work alone and draw the item.

Step 2 Hide Object

The object is placed out of sight. If it is displayed digitally, the projector or whiteboard is turned off. If it is a tangible item, it is covered up or placed under the desk so no one may see it.

Step 3 Teammates Share Drawings

Students take turns RoundRobin sharing their drawings with teammates.

Step 4 Objects Returned

After each teammate has shared his or her drawing, the team signals they are done. When everyone is ready, the object is returned to view.

Step 5 Students RoundRobin New Ideas

Students look again at the item and take turns stating ideas about what they did not have in their drawing. This pushes students to look at the item from a new or more detailed perspective. As teammates suggest new ideas, students may make notes.

Step 6 Students Improve Drawings

Students can improve their drawings by adding ideas they heard from teammates and/or elaborating on their notes from the second RoundRobin.

Observe-Write-RoundRobin

CHEMICAL REACTIONS
Observe-Write-RoundRobin

Teacher Instructions. Display one chemical reaction for the class to observe and describe in writing.

$H_2 + Cl_2 \longrightarrow 2HCl$

$2H_2 + O_2 \longrightarrow 2H_2O$

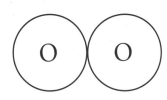

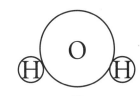

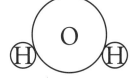

PAIRS COMPARE

PAIRS COMPARE

Pairs generate a list of possible ideas or answers, compare their answers with another pair, and then work as a team to create additional answers or ideas.

THE TEACHER presents a challenge to the class. The challenge can be a problem-solving challenge: *"How many ways can you build the number 12?"* Or the challenge can be an open-ended, brainstorming question to which creative ideas may be the solution: *"What are possible ways to reduce poverty?"* The important part is that there are multiple possible answers. Shoulder partners RallyTable ideas, passing a list back and forth, adding ideas. After the pairs have had some time to generate their own lists, the team unites and Pair A and Pair B compare lists. As a team the pairs do a RoundRobin, each in turn announcing one idea from the pair's list. The person from the other pair sitting across from the person who announces the item does one of two things: If his or her pair has something the same or similar, he or she checks it off, and, if not, adds it to the list. The Pairs Compare step continues until both pairs have shared all items and both pairs have identical lists. In the last step of this structure, the Team Challenge, all four teammates work together to see if they can come up with even more ideas to add to the lists. Partner A in each pair records the first new item, Partner B records the next, and so on, in a RallyTable format.

Pairs Compare is a strong structure for developing team synergy because teams are challenged to come up with new ideas based on the work of the pairs.

DIFFERENTIATED INSTRUCTION

• Nonwriters can be paired with a buddy who can act as Recorder.
• Students needing extra time or practice on the content can be given individual or group tutoring prior to Pairs Compare.
• Students can be given key words from which to draw.

BENEFITS

Students...

…are responsible for coming up with answers or ideas.

…hear ideas or answers from others.

…generate many possible answers.

…are challenged to come up with additional solutions as a team.

…take turns, keeping everyone actively engaged.

Step 1 — Teacher Asks Question

The teacher asks or provides a question that has multiple possible responses and provides Think Time. *"How has the Internet changed life as we know it? Think Time."* The prompt can also be completing a graphic organizer like a Venn diagram. *"Compare and contrast a plant cell and animal cell."*

Step 2 — RallyTable Answers

Shoulder partners RallyTable answers, passing the paper and pencil back and forth as they take turns writing their answers. They keep their answers a "secret" from the other pair.

Step 3 — Teacher Calls, "Time"

After pairs have recorded a number of responses, the teacher announces that time's up. *"Time's up! Pairs Compare."*

Step 4 — Pairs Compare

Pairs pair up with the other pair on their team. They RoundRobin their answers. For each answer, the face partner in the other pair adds the answer to that pair's list or checks it off if they already had it. When pairs are done comparing lists, both pairs have identical lists.

Step 5 — Team Challenge

The challenge is for teams to come up with new ideas that neither pair alone had generated. During this step, partners take turns recording each new idea generated by the team, no matter who came up with the idea.

Pairs Compare

STRUCTURE POWER

What is synergy? Synergy is the energy released from synthesis. Two plus two interacting are more than four. On tasks like generating ideas or evaluating ideas, individuals interacting produce a better result that even the best individual among them can produce alone. Each of us has our own knowledge base and our own point of view. All of us are smarter than any one of us. Pairs Compare is the embodiment of synergy. First, students work in pairs bouncing ideas off each other. The idea generated by one partner helps the other partner think of an idea he or she would not otherwise have come up with. This is synergy. Then the ideas are shared with the other pair. Because each pair has taken the task in a somewhat different direction, the ideas of one pair stimulates the other pair to think in fresh ways. Synergy is doubled! Finally, in the ultimate stimulus for synergy, the team is challenged to come up with ideas neither pair working alone had produced. Pairs Compare is synergy in action!

TIPS

• **Time It.** Give students a predetermined time to brainstorm their ideas in pairs and a second time limit for the team challenge.

• **Partners Record Ideas.** As pairs generate ideas, students can record their partners' ideas to promote listening.

• **Uneven Teams.** If there are one, two, or three students left over that don't fit into a group of four, send them each to a different team of four to form up to three teams of five. During pair work, in the teams of five, a pair and a triad are formed.

• **Many Possibilities.** It is important to provide a task that is open-ended. That is, there are many possible ideas or solutions. Otherwise, students may struggle to come up with ideas or may run out of things to add.

IDEAS Across the Curriculum

Mathematics
- Given item prices, write word problems
- All the ways to write the number 12
- Topics to gather data from charts, tables, or graphs
- Likely or unlikely events
- Fractions in real life
- Word problems for 3 + 4 − 2

Language Arts
- Write similes, metaphors, or analogies
- Mental images from a passage
- Remember events from a story
- Ideas for new endings
- Identify the most difficult words
- Adjectives to describe…
- Proper nouns
- Words that begin with the letter S
- Sentence fragments
- Examples of the use of a colon

Social Studies
- Opinions on various issues
- Advantages of a multicultural country
- Inventions that improved quality of life
- List the daily uses of money
- What you have learned about another country
- Presidents
- Laws
- Community helpers
- Roles of the government
- Things that change with time

Science
- Things that happen in a season
- Vertebrates or invertebrates
- Characteristics that are passed on from parent to offspring
- Impact of humans on environment

Music
- How the world would be different without music
- Bands
- Musicians
- Instruments
- Types of music
- Events where music is frequent

Teambuilding
- A good friend is...
- Things we have in common
- Vacation spots
- Good pets
- Favorite rides
- Fun weekend ideas
- Cartoon characters

Second Language
- Things in a refrigerator

Pairs Compare

VARIATIONS

• Pairs Compare for Problem Solving

Instead of using Pairs Compare to generate a list, use Pairs Compare for problem solving. Select problems which may be solved in a variety of ways or may have a number of possible answers or ideas. Pairs compare their answers in turn and the Team Challenge is to come up with solutions to the problem that neither pair alone had thought of.

• Graphic Organizers.

The simplest way to record ideas is a list. Pairs Compare may be made more sophisticated by providing graphic organizers. The key for using graphic organizers is the prompt must be open for many responses. For example, a timeline may work, but a step organizer with five steps won't.

RELATED STRUCTURE

#26 Teams Compare

Students work together in their teams to generate answers using RoundTable or Jot Thoughts. Teams then pair up with another team. As a group of eight, students RoundRobin answers their team generated. For each answer, a different teammate from the listening team adds the answer to his or her team list or checks it off if the team already has it. When all answers are shared, teams are challenged to work together to generate additional answers that neither team had generated.

Step 1 — Teacher Provides Question

The teacher provides a question that has multiple possible responses.

Step 2 — Teams Generate Answers

Teams generate multiple answers using RoundTable or Jot Thoughts.

Step 3 — Teams Pair Up

Teams pair up with another team.

Step 4 — Students RoundRobin Answers

As a group of eight, students RoundRobin answers its team generated. For each answer, a teammate from the listening team adds the answer to his or her team list or checks it off if the team already has it.

Step 5 — Teams Work Together

Team Challenge: When all answers are shared, teams are challenged to work together to generate additional answers that neither team had generated.

QUALITIES OF A GOOD TEAMMEMBER

Pairs Compare

Instructions. In pairs, take turns listing all the qualities of a good teammember. Compare your list with another pair and see if you came up with the same answers. Then, as a team of four, see if you can all come up with new ideas.

_____   _____

_____   _____

_____   _____

_____   _____

_____   _____

_____   _____

_____   _____

_____   _____

_____   _____

_____   _____

_____   _____

_____   _____

_____   _____

_____   _____

_____   _____

Are these qualities that you have? What can you work on?

VENN DIAGRAM
Pairs Compare

Instructions. Use this Venn diagram to compare and contrast. Write the titles on the lines provided.

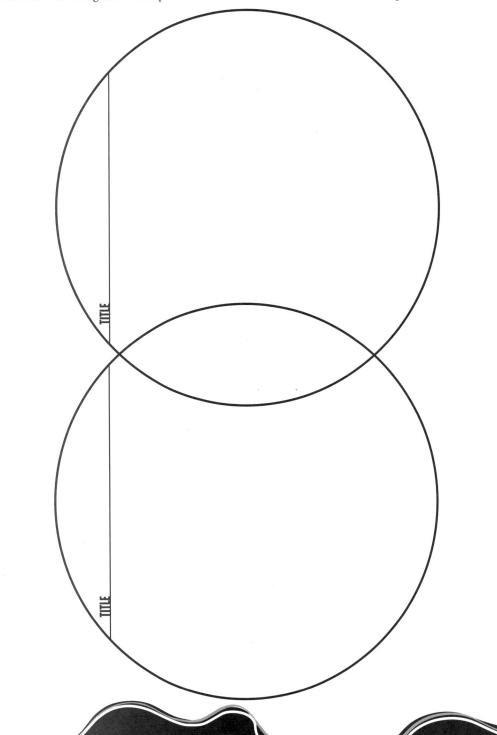

TITLE

TITLE

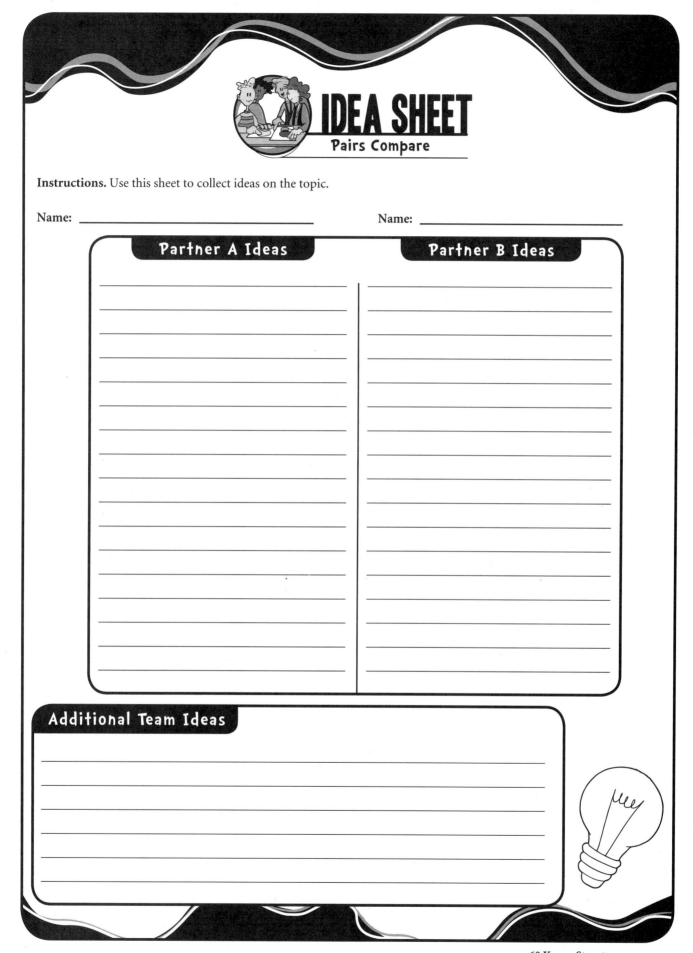

IDEA SHEET
Pairs Compare

Instructions. Use this sheet to collect ideas on the topic.

Name: _____   Name: _____

Partner A Ideas	Partner B Ideas

Additional Team Ideas

STORY PLOT TIMELINE
Pairs Compare

Instructions. Use this timeline to record the events that occurred in the story.

STORY PLOT TIMELINE

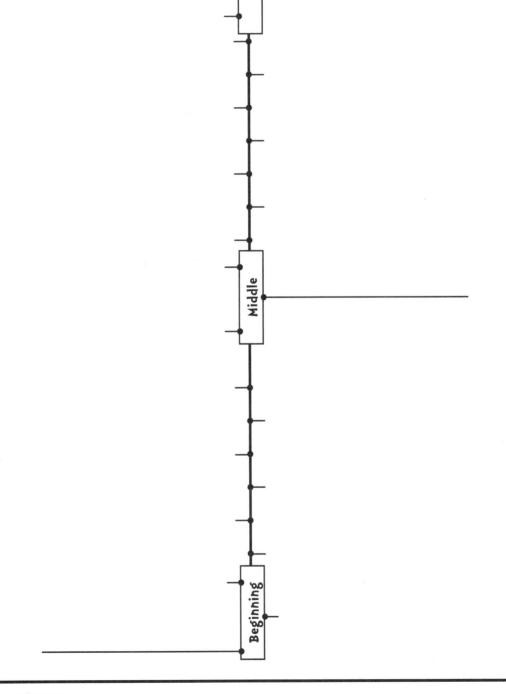

End

Middle

Beginning

Structure # 27

PARTNER STAR

Structure # 27
PARTNER STAR

In pairs, one partner is selected to be the "Star." The Star shares his or her answer with the other partner.

STEPS

Getting Ready

The teacher prepares questions or problems. Students pair up as A and B partners.

Step 1
Teacher Asks Question

The teacher asks or displays a question or problem. The question can be a review question, thinking question, or even a fun question. For example, *"Define the word hegemony."* Or, *"If you have traveled 2/9 of a trip of 81 miles, how far have you traveled?"* Or, *"What are the sequence of colors in the visible light spectrum?"* Or, *"Why do you think people reenact Civil War battles?"* Or, *"What did you do on the Fourth of July?"*

Step 2
Think Time

The teacher gives the class Think Time. *"Think about your answer."*

Step 3
Teacher Selects Partner

The teacher randomly picks Partner A or Partner B to be the star and to share. *"Partner A, you are the star! Please share your answer with your partner."*

Step 4
Partner Shares Answer

The selected student in each pair shares with his or her partner. *"The answer is 18 miles."* Or, *"We went to the beach and watched the fireworks show…"*.

Step 5
Teacher Reveals Answer

For right/wrong questions, the teacher reveals the correct answer. *"The answer is 18 miles. If your partner answered correctly, please give your partner a praiser. If your partner got a different answer, please show your partner how to solve the problem."*

Partner Star

RELATED STRUCTURE

#28 Traveling Pair Review

For Traveling Pair Review, students pair up with different classmates to do Pair Review. Students stand up, put a hand up, and pair up. The teacher asks the review question and provides some Think Time. The teacher then picks a partner to share. For example, *"Shorter partner, please share with your partner the connection between calorie restriction and life span."* After the selected partner shares, the teacher reveals the answer. The other student praises or coaches his or her partner. Then students put a hand up and "travel" to find a new partner.

Getting Ready
The teacher prepares review questions or problems.

Step 1 Students Stand Up, Hand Up, Pair Up

Students pair up with a classmate doing StandUp–HandUp–PairUp.

Step 2 Teacher Displays Question

The teacher asks or displays a review question or problem.

Step 3 Think Time

The teacher gives the class Think Time. *"Think about your answer."* Or, if it is a problem to solve, time to work out the answer.

Step 4 Partner Is Chosen to Share

The teacher picks a partner to share. *"Partner A, share your answer with your partner."*

Step 5 Selected Student Shares

The selected student in each pair shares with his or her partner.

Step 6 Teacher Reveals Answer

The teacher reveals the correct answer.

Step 7 Partners Praise or Coach

If the student is correct, his or her partner praises. *"That's right! High five!"* If the answer is incorrect, his or her partner coaches, then praises.

Step 8 Find a New Partner

Students "travel" to a new partner for each review question.

PICKING STICKIES

Structure # 29
PICKING STICKIES

Students pick stickies off their classmates for classbuilding, mastery, or higher-level thinking.

STEPS Getting Ready
Students need sticky notes or slips of paper with tape.

Step 2 Students Write

Students write their questions and/or answers on sticky notes. For mastery questions, the question is on the front and the answer is on the back.

Step 1 Teacher Announces Topic

The teacher announces a topic. For example, the topic may be explorers. The teacher asks students to write questions about the topic. The questions can be review questions, *"Write questions reviewing what we learned about explorers, each on a separate sticky note. Write the answer on the back."* Or the questions can be thinking questions, *"Write thinking questions about explorers, each on a separate sticky note. For example, 'Did Columbus really discover America if people already lived here?'"*

Picking Stickies can also be played for classbuilding. The teacher asks a question to which students write multiple responses, each on a separate sticky note. For example, *"What sports do you enjoy playing?"*

Step 3 Students Attach Stickies

Students attach stickies to a clipboard, sheet of paper, AnswerBoard, or to their own bodies.

Step 4 · Students Pair Up

Students stand up, put a hand up, and high five to pair up with a classmate.

Step 5 · Partners Take Turns

Partner A picks a sticky note from Partner B. What Partner B does next depends on the type of activity:

- **Classbuilding:** Partner B reads the sticky note. If it is true for him or her, Partner B takes it. For example, *"I take this… I also like playing soccer."*
- **Mastery:** Partner B reads the review question and responds. If correct, Partner A praises Partner B and Partner B takes the sticky note.
- **Thinking:** Partner B reads the thinking question and responds. Partner A praises the response and Partner B takes the sticky note.

Next, Partner A picks a sticky note from Partner B and responds accordingly.

Step 6 · Continue Pairing

Students continue pairing up, each time with a different classmate.

Step 7 · Return to Teams

After multiple pairings, the teacher announces that time is up and tells students to return to their teams. *"OK, thank your partner and return to your teams."*

Picking Stickies

FUN QUESTIONS
Picking Stickies

Teacher Instructions. Pick one of these questions to play Picking Stickies.

- **What are sports you enjoy playing?**

- **What are your favorite fast food restaurants?**

- **What are cartoons you like watching?**

- **What are your favorite Web sites?**

- **What are your favorite apps?**

- **Where are places you have been?**

- **Who are some of your favorite musicians?**

- **What video games or board games do you enjoy?**

- **What kind of fruit do you like eating?**

- **What are your hobbies?**

- **What movies have you seen that you enjoyed?**

Structure # 30

Q & A REVIEW

Structure # 30
Q & A REVIEW

Pairs review for a test or master the curriculum by first reading a question and answer and then asking a partner the question and having the partner restate the answer in his or her own words.

STEPS

Getting Ready
The teacher prepares a sheet with written questions and answers. Test-like questions with elaborated written responses work best.

Step 1 — Partner A Reads Q & A

Partner A reads the question and the answer to Partner B. Partner B listens very carefully. For example:

Q: *How is a lunar eclipse caused?*
A: *A lunar eclipse occurs when the moon passes behind the earth so that the earth blocks the sun's rays from striking the moon. This can occur only when the sun, earth, and moon are aligned with the earth in the middle.*

After reading the Q & A, Partner A reads just the question.
Q: *How is a lunar eclipse caused?*

Step 2 — Partner B Answers

Partner B flips over his or her sheet so he or she cannot see the answer, and then responds to the question in his or her own words.

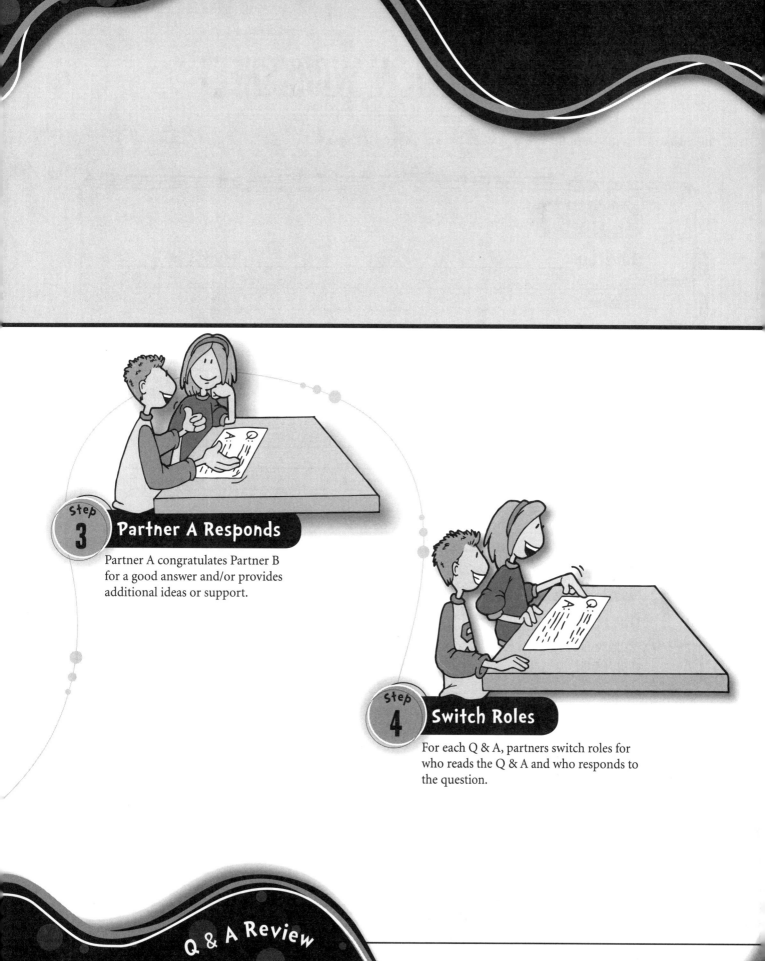

Step 3 — Partner A Responds

Partner A congratulates Partner B for a good answer and/or provides additional ideas or support.

Step 4 — Switch Roles

For each Q & A, partners switch roles for who reads the Q & A and who responds to the question.

Q & A Review

REVIEW WORKSHEET
Q & A Review

Instructions. Use this worksheet to prepare questions and answers for review.

Partner A

Question _____

_____

Answer _____

_____

_____

Partner B

Question _____

Answer _____

_____

_____

Partner A

Question _____

Answer _____

_____

_____

Partner B

Question _____

Answer _____

_____

_____

60 Kagan Structures
Kagan Publishing • 800.933.2667 • KaganOnline.com

Structure # 31

RAPPIN' TEAMS

Structure # 31
RAPPIN' TEAMS

Teams use rhyme, rhythm, repetition, and/or sound effects to create and perform a rap.

STEPS

Step 1
Teacher Assigns Rap Topic

The teacher assigns, or teams choose, the rap topic. Each team can have the same rap topic, or each team can be assigned a different topic that relates to the unit of study.

Step 2
Teams Generate Key Words

Teammates use AllRecord RoundRobin to generate and record a list of eight key words. For example, if the topic is DNA, then some of the key words may include cytosine, bases, double helix, and so on. Each teammate states one key word and all teammates record it.

Step 3
Teams Generate Rhyming Words

When the team has a solid list of key words, it then comes up with three or four rhyming words for each key word. For example, for the first key word cytosine, three rhyming words may include guanine, adenine, and thymine. All teammates record each word.

60 Kagan Structures
Kagan Publishing • 800.933.2667 • KaganOnline.com

Step 4 Teams Create Raps

Using the key words, rhyming words, and meter, teammates work together to create lines for their rap.

cytosine!

guanine!

Step 5 Teams Prepare Raps

Teammates practice their rap, deciding roles for each teammate. For example, they decide which teammates will sing which lines and which teammates might add verbal sound effects, clapping, or stomping.

Step 6 Team Up! to Share Raps

Teams team up. One team performs its rap for another team. The audience team responds, and then the teams switch roles.

Rappin' Teams

VARIATIONS

• **Class Presentations.** Teams can share their raps with the entire class. This takes longer than teams sharing with another team and fewer students are engaged, so it isn't recommended for each time.

• **Team-2-Team.** Use Team-2-Team to have teams share raps with multiple teams. Half the teams in the class spread around the perimeter of the class. The other half of the teams face them. Teams take turns sharing their raps. Then, the teams who presented first rotate to a new partner team to share again.

RELATED STRUCTURE

#32 Rappin' Pairs

Students create raps in pairs instead of in teams. They use Both Record RallyRobin for generating the key words and the rhyming words. When done, they share their raps with other pairs.

Step 1

Choose Rap Topic

The teacher assigns, or pairs choose, the rap topic.

Step 2

Partners Generate Key Words

Partners generate key words using Both Record RallyRobin: Partners take turns stating a key word and both record it.

Step 3

Partners Write Lines

Partners take turns writing lines using key words.

Step 4

Partners Create Couplets

Partners create couplets. They select a written line and then write a rhyming line that has the same meter and completes the verse.

Step 5

Partners Sequence Couplets

Partners sequence the couplets into a rap.

Step 6

Partners Practice

Partners practice their rap.

Step 7

Pairs Perform

Pairs perform their raps for another pair and/or for the class.

KEY WORDS
Rappin' Teams

Instructions. Come up with a list of eight key words on the topic. For each key word, generate three or four rhyming words.

Key Words	Rhyming Words			
1 _____	_____	_____	_____	_____
2 _____	_____	_____	_____	_____
3 _____	_____	_____	_____	_____
4 _____	_____	_____	_____	_____
5 _____	_____	_____	_____	_____
6 _____	_____	_____	_____	_____
7 _____	_____	_____	_____	_____
8 _____	_____	_____	_____	_____

RAP LINES
Rappin' Teams

Instructions. Record the key words your team brainstormed. Then use the rhyming words to come up with lines for your team rap.

Key Word: _____

Rap Line(s): _____

_____

_____

_____

_____

Key Word: _____

Rap Line(s): _____

_____

_____

_____

_____

Key Word: _____

Rap Line(s): _____

_____

_____

_____

_____

Kagan Publishing • 800.933.2667 • KaganOnline.com

READ-N-TELL!

Structure # 33
READ-N-TELL!

Partners take turns reading and summarizing material to boost comprehension and retention.

STEPS

Getting Ready

Students pair up. The teacher selects Partner A or B to start and tells the class how much or how long students are to read before their partner summarizes what was just read—after each paragraph, after every 3 minutes (or selected time), after every page, or after every section.

Step 1 — Partner A Reads

Partner A reads aloud for the allotted time or through the assigned section while Partner B listens.

Step 2 — Partner B Summarizes

Partner B summarizes the reading to Partner A without referring to the text. *"The main character just confronted the antagonist…"*.

Step 3 — Partner B Reads

Partner B reads to Partner A.

Step 4 · Partner A Summarizes

Partner A summarizes the reading to Partner B.

Step 5 · Continue Reading

Partners continue taking turns, one reading for the allotted time or assigned section and the other summarizing what he or she heard from his or her partner.

Read-N-Tell!

SUMMARIZING GAMBITS
Read-N-Tell

Teacher Instructions. Display these gambits for students to use as they summarize the reading.

- To summarize…

- The main idea is…

- I just heard…

- You just read…

- We just learned…

ROVING REPORTER

Structure #34
ROVING REPORTER

While working on projects, teams send out a Roving Reporter or scout to gather and bring back information to help the team.

STEPS Getting Ready
Students work on team projects.

Step 1 Select Roving Reporter

The teacher or teams select a Roving Reporter. The Roving Reporter can be randomly chosen with the spin of a Student Selector Spinner by the teacher or the team, or the team can pick a teammate to rove and report. *"Student #2 on each team has been selected to be the Roving Reporter."*

Step 2 Teacher Announces Time Limit

The teacher announces a time limit for roving. For example, *"Roving Reporters, you will have 3 minutes to rove the classroom and browse other projects. Take careful notes and/or make sketches because you will share what you learned with your team when you return."*

Step 3 Rovers Observe

The Roving Reporters rove through the classroom and observe the projects of other teams. Teammates continue working on their projects.

Step 4 — Teacher Calls Time

When time's up, the teacher calls time. *"Time's up. Roving Reporters, please make your way back to your team and sit down."*

Step 5 — Rovers Report

The Roving Reporters return to their teams. The team stops working, focuses on the Roving Reporter, and the Roving Reporter shares information he or she gathered. *"Share the information you gathered with your teammates and discuss what ideas, if any, you'd like to incorporate in your own project."*

Roving Reporter vs. One Stray

Roving Reporters can visit a number of teams, choosing which teams to visit. The goal of the Roving Reporters is to gather information to bring back to their team, usually information about how other teams are designing their projects. In contrast, in One Stray, students visit just one other team and their goal is either to share information or to gather information.

Roving Reporter

ROVING REPORTER FORM

Roving Reporter

Instructions. Use this form to make sketches and take notes about team projects you'd like to report to your team.

Sketch Here

Report Back_____
_____
_____
_____
_____

Sketch Here

Report Back_____
_____
_____
_____
_____

Sketch Here

Report Back_____
_____
_____
_____
_____

Sketch Here

Report Back_____
_____
_____
_____
_____

Structure # 35

SAME-DIFFERENT

Structure # 35
SAME-DIFFERENT

Pairs discover attributes that are the same and different in two pictures or objects. The challenge: Neither partner can see the other's item.

STUDENTS PAIR UP. A barrier is placed between the pair. Each pair receives two pictures or items that have a number of similarities and a number of differences. Partners hide their pictures or items from each other behind a barrier. The two items can be identical pictures with the exception of missing, modified, colored, moved, or added details. Or the two items can be two newspaper articles on the same subject written by different authors, two versions of the same song, or a plastic model of a zebra and a horse. The pair's task is to find all the similarities and differences between the two items. The challenge is that neither partner can see what the other's looks like, so they must be very analytic in their examination of their items and precise in their verbal descriptions. Partners take turns recording the similarities and differences. After the pair thinks it has uncovered all the similarities and differences, it compares the items to see how well it did. The pair checks to make sure everything it listed is accurate, and it continues to find more similarities and differences.

Same-Different is terrific for developing analytic skills and oral communication skills. It offers a wonderful forum to carefully analyze any learning material.

DIFFERENTIATED INSTRUCTION

- Selected pairs may be given simpler or more complex pictures.
- Selected pairs may have the opportunity to view pictures before playing.
- Some players may be allowed to talk, write, and draw on notes while others may have limited communication channels such as draw only.

BENEFITS

Students...

...develop perspective taking as they must imagine themselves in the role of the other.

...develop strong verbal communication skills as they must describe what the other can't see.

...develop analytic skills as they carefully examine their own items.

...reach a shared goal with a partner through cooperation and coordinating efforts.

...develop vocabulary based on the item.

...develop many of their intelligences while engaged.

Getting Ready

Barriers are placed between partners. Partners each receive a different picture or item placed out of view of their partner. The two items are the same in some ways and different in others. Partners also need one recording sheet that has a column for "Same" and a column for "Different" and a pen or pencil.

STEPS

Step 1 — Partner A Describes Item

Partners examine their respective items and try to uncover what is the "Same" and what is "Different" in two pictures or objects. Partner A starts: *"My possum only has seven stripes. Does yours have seven stripes?"*

Step 2 — Partners Take Turns Recording

If the item is the same, Partner B writes the similarity in the "Same" column of the recording sheet. If it is different, Partner B records the difference in the "Different" column. Using RallyTable, partners take turns recording the similarities and differences on the recording sheet.

Step 3 — Partner B Describes Item

Partner B now shares a feature of his or her item: *"My snake is coiled three times. Is yours?"*

Step 4 — Partners Compare Items

When time's up or when the pair thinks it has uncovered all the similarities and differences, the pair places them side by side and examines them. The partners then review their lists for accuracy and write additional similarities or differences.

Same-Different

STRUCTURE POWER

Students rise to the challenge of finding what is the same and what is different in the two objects when they each can see only one. The content itself can be quite instructive; for example, students can learn about similarities and differences between a butterfly and a moth. Perhaps more important are the skills that are acquired as students play the game. Analytic thinking is a major part of the IQ test—scores on several IQ scales depend on the ability to analyze and to break a whole into its components. Same-Different trains analytic thinking because the road to success is to examine details. Perspective taking—ability to take the role of others, understanding another mind—is a social skill critical to the development of empathy, cooperation, conflict resolution, and caring for others. Same-Different is training in the ability to take the role of others; students learn that what they see is not what their partner sees. Communication skills are enhanced as well. Students learn to describe with precision what they see. They learn to check for understanding and to seek clarification. This is the power of Same-Different; while playing a game they love, students are acquiring some of the most essential skills: analytic skills, perspective-taking skills, and communication skills!

TIPS

• **File Folder Barriers.** File folder barriers are very simple to build. Give each pair two file folders and one paper clip. The pair clips the file folders together at the top with a paper clip, spreads the base, and presto! The partners have a stand alone buddy barrier.

• **More Barriers.** Other possible barriers include an open textbook, a three-ring binder, or a cardstock barrier.

• **Back-to-Back.** Instead of using buddy barriers, you can also have pairs work back-to-back on the floor.

• **Storing Barriers.** When done with Same-Different, have students fold down their barriers and secure the pictures (if they used pictures) inside with the paper clip.

• **Sponge Activity.** Pairs will finish at different rates. Have other items available or another activity prepared such as writing a compare and contrast essay about the items.

• **Possible Materials.** Same-Different can be played with a number of materials. Try Same-Different with pictures, articles, advertisements, foods, soft drink cans, music, rocks, plants, materials, books, problems, or films.

• **Reflection Time.** Interrupt students after a few minutes of playing. Ask them to reflect on what roles and strategies they are using, what is being effective, and what is not working.

• **Communication Skills.** Teach students two key communication skills: checking for understanding and asking for clarification. Have them generate or provide gambits for each skill. Checking for understanding: *"Did you understand that my picture has only…"* Asking for clarification: *"Do you mean that your picture has…"*.

IDEAS Across the Curriculum

Mathematics
- Compass and protractor
- Two diagrams
- Two word problems
- Two groups of numbers
- Two geometric shapes
- Two sets of data
- Two graphs (line, pie, bar, or pictograph)

Language Arts
- Two characters of a story
- Two short stories
- Friendly letter vs. business letter
- Two fairy tale pictures

Social Studies
- Two historical figures
- Two time periods
- Two maps
- Two state descriptions
- Different descriptions of the same event
- Different descriptions of the same person
- Two holiday pictures

Science
- Two similar animals
- Two insects
- Two flowers
- Fresh water and salt water
- Sun and moon
- Two fossils
- Two rocks or minerals
- Saturn and Jupiter
- Bird wing and fish fin
- Animal cell and plant cell

Music
- Two versions of the same song
- Two similar compositions
- Two musicians
- Different instruments

Art
- Two pictures of the same subject matter by different artists
- Two self-portraits by the same artist
- Two pictures from different angles
- Two different periods
- Lives of two artists

Same-Different

VARIATIONS

• **Team Same-Different.** Same-Different may be played with two students on each side of the barrier. Same-side pairs take turns (RallyRobin) describing their items and recording the similarities and differences (RallyTable).

• **Other Ways to Communicate.** Partners may communicate in any of the following ways:

• **Passing Notes.** Students write their observations or questions on a slip of paper and pass notes up and back to uncover similarities and differences.

• **Detailed Descriptions.** Students write a detailed description of their item and then give their description to their partner. The other student must use the written description to list similarities and differences. This promotes descriptive writing.

• **Act It Out.** Students act out the features of their items without talking.

• **Hide It.** Give students 2 minutes to examine their item, take notes, and make sketches. When the time is up, students hide their items and play Same-Different using only their notes.

• **From Memory.** Students study the pictures for 1 minute, then hide their pictures. They then play from memory.

• **Sketch It.** Students have a limited time to sketch their picture or object. They then trade drawings and play Same-Different using only their drawings.

• **Class Same-Different.** For younger students, try Same-Different with the entire class. Half the class has access to one picture or item and the other half to another item. The whole class works together to find similarities and differences.

• **No Barrier.** For very young students, don't use a barrier; give each team two items. The team's task is to find the similarities and differences as a pair sitting side by side.

• **Friendly Competition.** Pairs are given a limited amount of time and must find as many similarities and differences as possible. The pair with the most points wins. The pair's prize is to share with the class their method of working so efficiently.

TROPICAL RAIN FOREST (Picture 1)
Same-Different

Instructions. Find items that are the same and different in Picture 1 and Picture 2.

SOURCE: Candler, L. *Exploring the Rain Forest.* San Clemente, CA: Kagan Publishing.

TROPICAL RAIN FOREST (Picture 2)
Same-Different

Instructions. Find items that are the same and different in Picture 1 and Picture 2.

SOURCE: Candler, L. *Exploring the Rain Forest.* San Clemente, CA: Kagan Publishing.

RECORDING SHEET
Same-Different

Instructions. Record items that are the same and different.

Same	Different
1. _____	1. _____
2. _____	2. _____
3. _____	3. _____
4. _____	4. _____
5. _____	5. _____
6. _____	6. _____
7. _____	7. _____
8. _____	8. _____
9. _____	9. _____
10. _____	10. _____
11. _____	11. _____
12. _____	12. _____
13. _____	13. _____
14. _____	14. _____
15. _____	15. _____
16. _____	16. _____
17. _____	17. _____
18. _____	18. _____
19. _____	19. _____
20. _____	20. _____

Structure # 36

SHARE-N-SWITCH

Structure # 36
SHARE-N-SWITCH

After sharing with their shoulder partners, students turn to share with their face partners. Share-N-Switch gives students the opportunity to hear from different teammates, the chance to integrate new ideas, and the forum for elaborating on ideas.

STEPS
Getting Ready
The teacher prepares the discussion topic.

Step 1
Teacher Announces Topic

The teacher announces a discussion topic to the class. For example, *"Which invention had the biggest impact and why?"* A variation is students may think and write before they share. *"Write which invention had the biggest impact and why."*

Step 2
Shoulder Partners Share

Using Timed Pair Share, students take timed turns sharing with their shoulder partners. Partner A shares for 30 seconds (or the predetermined time limit) while Partner B listens. Then Partner B shares while Partner A listens.

VARIATION

- **RallyTable-N-Switch.** Students make a list or build a project with their shoulder partner and then switch to continue the work with their face partner. For example, students have done a RallyTable with their shoulder partners listing random acts of kindness they could do. Then, at a signal from the teacher, they turn to their face partners. Face partners each have one list. At a second signal from the teacher, they continue adding to the list they have using RallyTable with their face partner.

Step 3 — Face Partners Share

Students now pair up with their face partners and use Timed Pair Share to share again on the same topic.

Share-N-Switch vs. Sharing Secrets

Share-N-Switch is two consecutive Timed Pair Shares on the same topic, first with their shoulder partner then with their face partner. When speaking a second time on the same topic, students elaborate and become more fluent in their speech and ideation. In contrast, Sharing Secrets is two consecutive Timed Pair Interviews, first with their shoulder partner and then with their face partner. It is an opportunity for students to practice their interviewing skills and to summarize what they have learned in an interview.

Share-N-Switch

DISCUSSION TOPICS
Share-N-Switch

Teacher Instructions. Try Share-N-Switch with one of these discussion topics.

Hobbies

• What are hobbies you enjoy? When do you do them?
Who do you do them with?

Music

• What type of music do you like? Who is your favorite musician?
What do you like about him/her/them?

Careers

• If you could do anything as a career, what would you do? Why?

Food

• What is your favorite dinner? Favorite restaurant?
Can you cook?

Sports

• What is your favorite sport to play? When do you play?
Who do you play with? Why do you enjoy it?

Television

• What shows do you enjoy on TV? Why do you like them?
How often do you watch TV? Who do you watch TV with?

SHOW ME

Structure # 37
SHOW ME

Equilateral

Students all respond to a question by simultaneously displaying their responses.

STEPS

Getting Ready
Students each have a response board and marker.

Step 1
Teacher Asks Question

The teacher asks a question. For Show Me, the question is usually a short-answer question so the teacher may quickly assess students' responses by scanning the room. *"What type of triangle meets this definition: Three equal sides, three equal angles, or always 60 degrees."*

Step 2
Think Time

The teacher provides 3–5 seconds of Think Time. *"Think about your answer."*

Step 3
Students Write Answers

The teacher tells students to write their answers large. Students independently write their own answers on their own response boards. *"Please write your own answers on your response boards. Write large enough so I can see it!"*

Step 4 — Show Me

The teacher calls, *"Show me!"*

Equilateral

Step 5 — Students Display Responses

Students simultaneously hold up their response boards in front of their chests for the teacher to formatively assess the class. Holding them in front of their chests keeps the boards steady and prevents classmates from seeing each other's answers. The teacher shares the correct answer with the class. If many students had the wrong answer, the teacher may reteach the concept or provide practice opportunities.

Show Me

VARIATIONS

· Response Cards. Students select the correct response card, place it on the top of the stack, and hold the stack to their chest hiding the selected response card until the teacher calls, *"Show Me!"* The cards can be numbers or letters corresponding to a key. Or the cards can have actual responses. For this example, response cards would each have a different type of triangle: Equilateral, Isosceles, Scalene, and so on. They would hold up the card that corresponds to the answer. Keeping the cards in a stack prevents other teammates from seeing which responses were not chosen and thereby hides the chosen answers.

· Finger Responses. The number of fingers corresponds to the answer or to a key. To avoid copycat responses and promote individual accountability, have students show their fingers in front of their chests. This way the teacher can see the number, but classmates can't just follow the crowd or copy a classmate. For example, a finger key might look like this:
- 1 finger = mammal
- 2 fingers = reptile
- 3 fingers = bird
- 4 fingers = fish

"What type of animal is a dolphin. Show me!"

TRUE OR FALSE RESPONSE CARDS
Show Me

Instructions. Use these response cards for Show Me with true or false questions.

MULTIPLE-CHOICE RESPONSE CARDS
Show Me

Instructions. Use these response cards for Show Me with multiple-choice questions.

THE ANSWER IS...

A

THE ANSWER IS...

B

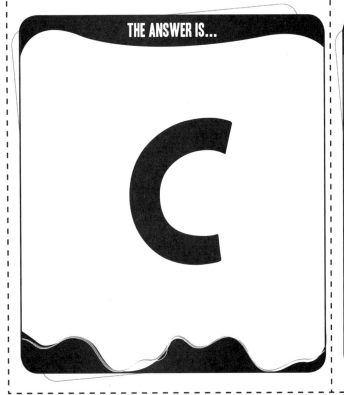

THE ANSWER IS...

C

THE ANSWER IS...

D

SPEND-A-BUCK

Structure # 38
SPEND-A-BUCK

To make a team decision, teammates use play dollars and "spend a buck" to make a selection from multiple alternatives.

THERE ARE TIMES when teams need to choose between alternatives. Teammates may pull in different directions as they attempt to reach consensus on a team name. Or a team may brainstorm multiple possible project ideas but can't reach consensus on which one to pursue. Or a team may be split on which of four story starters it wants to write about. Spend-A-Buck empowers teams to make decisions without creating winners and losers. First, each teammate receives 10 play dollars. Play money, tokens, slips of paper, counting chips, or any tangible items can be used to represent the dollars. There is one rule: Students must spend at least 1 buck on each alternative. Each teammate spends the rest of his or her money on the alternatives any way he or she pleases. After students spend their bucks, the team sums the money for each alternative. The alternative with the most bucks is deemed the team decision.

Since some money was spent on each alternative, all students feel their favorite received some support. It is not obvious how much each person advocated each item, so there are no losers. It feels like a team decision all can endorse.

BENEFITS

Students...

...make a team decision.

...evaluate alternatives.

...state their personal preferences.

Getting Ready

STEPS

Each teammate receives 10 play dollars. Alternatives to choose among (no more than four) are written on cards or slips of paper.

Step 1 — Alternatives Spread Out

The team spreads out the choice of alternatives on its team table. *"Spread out your alternatives so there is space between them and everyone can read each alternative."*

Step 2 — Teammates Spend One Buck

Teammates spend 1 dollar on each alternative by placing a buck on the alternative. *"Spend 1 buck on each alternative."*

Step 3 — Think Time

Students think about their personal preferences and how they want to spend the rest of their bucks.

Step 4 — Teammates Spend Rest

Teammates spend their remaining dollars any way they want by placing their bucks on their preferred alternative(s). *"When I say, "Go!" quickly spend the rest of your bucks any way you want. If you like two or more alternatives, you may want to spend some bucks on each. No holdouts allowed!"*

Step 5 — Teams Count Cash

Teams count the bucks spent on each alternative. The alternative with the most money is deemed the team decision.

Spend-A-Buck

STRUCTURE POWER

Spend-A-Buck is an alternative to voting. Voting polarizes; it creates winners and losers. And the losers are not likely to give full support to the decision they voted against. In contrast, with Spend-A-Buck there are no clear winners and losers; what emerges is a team decision. To each member it feels like: *"The weight of our feelings has been measured and we have decided on this alternative."* Everyone feels he or she can endorse the team decision; group unity has been strengthened. Spend-A-Buck is faster than prolonged consensus seeking and is useful when we want to make a quick decision so we can get to work. It promotes conflict avoidance, harmonious team relations, and evaluative thinking.

TIPS

- **Teacher Directed First.** The first few times students do Spend-A-Buck, lead the class through the steps. The ultimate goal is for students to consider Spend-A-Buck any time they need to make a team decision and to lead themselves through the decision-making process.

- **Tie Breakers.** To break a tie, the other alternatives are set aside. Students RoundRobin, making a case for their preferred alternative. The team plays Spend-A-Buck again with just the tied alternatives. If there's another tie, the team can flip a coin.

- **No Scale Tippers.** Students must all spend their bucks at the same time so no teammate can wait to see how teammates spend their money and tip the scales in his or her favor.

- **Limit the Alternatives.** If there are more than four alternatives, each teammate can select their favorite. When done, there are no more than four alternatives from which to choose.

- **Proactive Advocating.** Prior to Spend-A-Buck, have students do a RoundRobin, each in turn saying why they like one or more alternatives. The rule is no reactive or negative statements. Allowed: *"I favor ____ because…"* Not Allowed: *"____ is a bad choice because…"*.

Mathematics

Teams select...

- Best way to graph data
- Favorite tessellation
- Best real-world application
- Least likely answer
- Most likely answer

Language Arts

Teams select...

- Favorite book
- Favorite scene
- Who is the most influential author of the twentieth century
- Writing topic
- Favorite character sketch
- Sentence with the worst grammar/spelling
- Best moral of the story
- Best topic sentence
- Prediction of what will happen next in the story
- Next book/story to read
- Best summary
- Adjective that best describes the character

Social Studies

Teams select...

- American heroes
- Culture liked the most
- Decade they would most like to visit
- Biggest threat to humanity
- Team project topic
- Social issue to research
- Favorite political cartoon to share
- Best solution to a problem
- Side in a war/conflict

Science

Teams select...

- Most important invention
- Experiment they would want to do
- Team science project
- Most pressing ethical issue
- Experiment to conduct
- Hypothesis
- Animal to research
- Planet to research
- Inventor to research

Teambuilding

Teams select...

- Team name
- Team picture to post
- Field day activities
- Team logo
- Team project

Spend-A-Buck

VARIATIONS

• **Voting.** Voting is the traditional democratic decision-making procedure. Everyone casts one vote, and the alternative with the most votes wins. Voting, however, creates winners and losers. In the case of cooperative work, losers are less committed to team decisions based on a vote.

• **Class Spend-A-Buck.** The teacher posts the alternatives around the class. Each team has ten sticky notes, each representing a buck. The team must spend a buck on each alternative stating something positive about each alternative and reach consensus on how they will spend the remaining bucks. They spend their bucks by sticking the sticky notes to the alternatives they want to vote for. The teacher sums the bucks for each alternative, and the one with the most bucks is deemed the class decision.

SPEND-A-BUCK
Spend-A-Buck (Bucks)

Instructions. Cut out and use these "bucks" to play Spend-A-Buck.

SPEND-A-BUCK
Spend-A-Buck (Coins)

Instructions. Cut out and use these "coins" to play Spend-A-Buck.

Structure # 39

STANDUP – HANDUP – PAIRUP

Structure # 39
STANDUP—HANDUP—PAIRUP

Students stand up, put their hands up, and quickly find a classmate so they are ready to interact in pairs.

STANDUP—HANDUP—PAIRUP is a staple in any interactive classroom. It is one of the easiest ways to instantly create student engagement. It works exactly like its name suggests. Students stand up. They put a hand up, and then they pair up with the nearest classmate who is not a teammate. They give each other a high five, and then they lower their hands so everyone can tell they're not looking for a partner. Now that they're in pairs, partners are ready to interact.

Partners can interact in a number of ways. For example, they can do a RallyRobin taking turns responding to the teacher's prompt such as, "*Name things you did this weekend.*" They can do a Timed Pair Share where they each take an equal, timed turn to respond to the teacher's question such as, "*If you were in the same predicament as the main character, how would you react?*" Any way you use it, StandUp–HandUp–PairUp is a terrific structure for getting students up, out of their seats and interacting with their classmates.

BENEFITS

Students...

...discuss and interact with classmates.

...are energized by standing and pairing.

...form positive bonds with classmates.

...process what was just taught.

Step 1
Teacher Directs Class

The teacher tells the class to, "*Stand up, put a hand up, and pair up!*"

Step 2
Students Pair Up

Students stand up, put a hand up in the air, and keep it in the air until they find the closest partner who's not a teammate. They give each other a high five and lower their hands.

Step 3
Teacher Provides Topic and Think Time

The teacher asks the class a question or gives an assignment and provides Think Time. For example, *"What do you think the government should do to encourage alternate energy sources?"*

Step 4
Partners Interact

Partners interact using structures such as:
- **Timed Pair Share**–Partners take turns sharing for a predetermined time period.
- **RallyRobin**–Partners take turns stating possible answers, usually with multiple rounds.
- **RallyQuiz**–Partners take turns quizzing each other.

StandUp–HandUp–PairUp

STRUCTURE POWER

Two of the more important applications of brain science to the classroom are (1) the importance of creating novelty and (2) the importance of including movement because movement nourishes the brain. StandUp–HandUp–PairUp does both! The brain wakes up when faced with novel stimuli. If students interact with only their teammates, the class is a predictable world and brains are less alert. If, instead, at any moment students may be asked to interact with someone new from the class, their brains are immediately energized. The second important way in which StandUp–HandUp–PairUp is brain friendly is that it includes movement. Whenever there is major muscle movement, heart rate and volume increase as does breathing rate and volume. This means that the heart is pumping more blood to the brain (bringing more oxygen and glucose) but also, because of the increased breathing rate, the blood the heart is pumping has less CO_2 and more O_2. Thus StandUp–HandUp–PairUp wakes up the brain in two ways: providing novelty and providing more nutrients. Why would we choose to have the brains of our students less energized and less nourished when, in a few moments, they can be more fully prepared to learn? Yet another way in which StandUp–HandUp–PairUp is powerful: students love to move and interact. With this simple structure, we are allowing students to do two of the things they most want to do. No wonder students love classrooms that include StandUp–HandUp–PairUp.

TIPS

• **Think Time.** Remember to provide 3–5 seconds of Think Time before students share their responses with a partner.

• **Time It.** Use a timer when using Timed Pair Share to give each pair equal time.

• **Odd Number.** If you have an odd number of students in the class, join in or make one team of three.

• **No Passes.** When it is time for students to pair up, there is a rule that there is no passing anyone up. Students must pair with the closest person to them.

• **No Teammates.** When using StandUp–HandUp–PairUp for classbuilding, remember to tell the class that there is no pairing up with teammates.

• **Mix Up Share Modes.** For novelty and practice with the different types of responses, mix up share modes between Timed Pair Share, RallyRobin, and Timed Pair Interview.

• **Sticky High Five.** To pair up, students can do a "sticky high five." They give each other a high five but keep their hands stuck together. This keeps students facing each other and makes it easy for classmates to see who's already paired up.

• **Move to the Center.** As students pair up, it is helpful if students move toward the center of the classroom. That makes it quicker and easier to find a partner. If necessary, they can spread out once they find a partner.

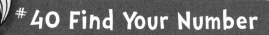

#40 Find Your Number

In teams, each student has a number 1 to 4. The teacher announces to the class, *"Find your number."* Students stand up and put a hand up. With their raised hands, they indicate their number by raising 1 to 4 fingers. Students look for a partner with the same number. For example, Student #3 looks for a partner with three fingers raised. When they find each other, partners do a high five and lower their hands to indicate they've found a partner. When all hands are down and students are in pairs, the teacher asks a question or provides a task for students to interact in pairs. One caution: if you have an odd number of teams in your class (say 7 teams), the class won't break evenly into same number pairs. Remaining students have to pair up with different number partners.

#41 Find A Different Number

Find A Different Number works the same as Find Your Number except that students can now pair up with any student except for a student with the same number. For example, Student #3s can't pair up with Student #3s. The potential problem about odd number teams for same number partners does not apply to different number partners, so this structure may be preferable if you have an odd number of teams in your class.

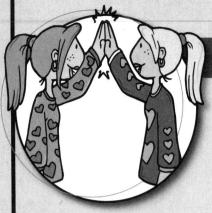

#42 Find Your Match

To have students pair up, the teacher announces a characteristic such as, *"Same color eyes, find your match."* Students must pair up with a classmate who matches them (or is similar) on the characteristic. If there are any unmatched students, they can pair up with anyone who hasn't yet found a match.

Matching Characteristics

Here are a few characteristics to have students find their match:

- Same height
- Same hair length
- Same colored shirt
- Same colored pants
- Same hair color
- Same eye color

- Similar birthday
- Same favorite color
- Same favorite sport
- Same or close first letter of first name
- Similar number of siblings

USA FUN FACTS
StandUp—HandUp—PairUp

Teacher Instructions. When students are in pairs, ask one question and have Partner A respond to Partner B. Then the students switch roles for the next question. Have students pair up with a different classmate for every two questions.

1 Which president served more than two terms?

2 Which state is Mount Rushmore located in?

3 What year did WWII begin?

4 What are the names of the three ships Christopher Columbus used on his voyage to America?

5 What is the capital of Florida?

6 Which amendment is the right to bear arms?

7 What is the time distance between California and New York?

8 When was the Declaration of Independence issued?

9 Which state is the 50th and most recent state to join the U.S.?

10 Which country did the U.S. purchase Alaska from?

11 Which region of the U.S. is known as "Tornado Alley?"

12 Which four states can you stand in at the same time?

Answers:
1. Franklin Delano Roosevelt **2.** South Dakota **3.** 1939 **4.** La Niña, La Pinta, and La Santa Maria **5.** Tallahassee **6.** Second
7. 3 hours **8.** July 4, 1776 **9.** Hawaii **10.** Russia **11.** The Midwest **12.** Arizona, Colorado, New Mexico, Utah

LISTS GALORE
StandUp–HandUp–PairUp

Teacher Instructions. Use these fun list topics to have students RallyTable ideas in pairs.

- Sports that are played with a ball
- Countries in the world
- Elements in the periodic table
- Cereal brands
- Famous athletes
- Types of cars
- Movies
- Cartoons

- Things in a house
- Things that are green
- Things that you might find in a rain forest
- Landforms
- Snacks
- Types of drinks
- Items of clothing
- Things in the sea
- Things that fly

SWITCH OR TRADE

Structure # 43
SWITCH OR TRADE

Students never know! Will the teacher call, "Switch" or "Trade?" Partners either switch who's doing the work or trade work with another pair.

STEPS Getting Ready

Shoulder partners are given an assignment such as a writing assignment or drawing.

Step 1
Partner A Begins

Partner A begins the assignment while Partner B watches, listens, and coaches.

Step 2
Teacher Calls Switch or Trade

At any time the teacher may call, *"Switch,"* or, *"Trade."*

Step 3 Students Switch or Trade

If the teacher calls, *"Switch,"* shoulder partners switch roles. If Partner A was doing the assignment, now it's Partner Bs turn. If the teacher calls, *"Trade,"* pairs trade papers with their face partners.

Step 4 Students Resume Work

When a student receives the paper from a face or shoulder partner, the student picks up where the last person left off. For example, if the task is writing a story, the student continues the story. If the task is writing a list (adjectives that describe a character), the student continues adding to the list. If the task is drawing or creating a visual organizer, the student takes over until the next switch or trade.

Switch or Trade

VARIATIONS

• **Trade Places.** Add novelty by trading places. Instead of just saying, *"Trade,"* the teacher can say, *"Partner As trade places."* Partner As switch seats so everyone has a new shoulder partner. The papers stay with Partner Bs, so each pair has a paper.

• **Switch and Trade.** If the teacher calls, *"Switch and Trade,"* pairs trade papers and partners switch roles.

Structure # 44

TAKEOFF – TOUCHDOWN

Structure #44
TAKEOFF—TOUCHDOWN

Students stand and sit to answer questions as the teacher polls the class.

STEPS

Getting Ready
The teacher prepares statements.

Step 1
Teacher Makes Statement

The teacher makes a statement. Some different types of statements include:
- True or false review statement – *"Perpendicular means two lines that never intersect."*
- Student knowledge – *"I can solve this type of problem." "I know the definition of …".*
- Student opinion – *"I agree with the president's decision."*
- Personal preference – *"I like chocolate better than vanilla."*
- Student attributes – *"I walk to school."*

Step 2
Students Take Off

Students stand up ("Take Off") or remain seated depending on their response. *"Take off if you agree."* Or, *"Take off if you think the answer is C."*

Step 3 Teacher Makes Next Statement

The teacher makes the next statement.

Step 4 Students Take Off or Touch Down

- **Standing students:** If the statement applies again, they remain standing. Otherwise, they sit down ("Touch Down").
- **Seated students:** If the statement now applies, they stand up. Otherwise, they remain seated.

TakeOff—TouchDown

RELATED STRUCTURE

#45 StepUp

StepUp is very similar to TakeOff–TouchDown. A strip of tape is placed on the floor. Half the class lines up parallel to the strip on one side of the tape strip, and the other half lines up parallel to the strip on the other side of the tape strip. Both sides take one large step back. The teacher makes a statement and students "step up" to the line if the statement applies to them. For example, *"I have been to Europe."* After students step up, they can be filtered out by having them stay if more specific statements apply to them. For example, *"Remain in the center if you have been to France. Remain in the center if you have been to Paris."* StepUp provides a good visual poll of the class.

Students Line Up
Students line up on both sides of the tape and take one large step back.

Tape

Students Step Up
Students step up to the middle if the statement is true for them.

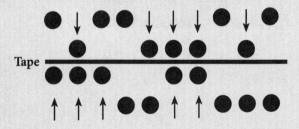

Tape

Teacher Makes Statement
The teacher makes a statement, *"Step up if you think seniors should be allowed to go off campus for lunch."*

Structure # 46

TEAM MIND-MAPPING

Structure # 46
TEAM MIND-MAPPING

Teammates work together to create a team mind map, symbolizing the content in a visual/spatial, relational format.

EACH TEAM receives a large sheet of butcher or chart paper. Each student has a different color pen, crayon, or marker. The teacher announces the mind-mapping topic. Just about any topic will work, but the best topics are ones that have many related details and connections. For social studies, it can be an historical event, a current event, a famous person, or a concept such as culture. For language arts, it can be a book, story, or character. For math, it can be an algorithm, a mathematical concept, or a mathematician. For science, it can be a unit topic, a scientific principle, or a scientist. One student writes the topic in the center of the paper. Using RoundTable Consensus, the team writes the core concepts around the main topic with lines connecting concepts to the main idea. When teams are satisfied with the core concepts, they do a free-for-all, adding supporting elements, drawing symbols, using colors, and writing key words to elaborate their mind map.

Team Mind-Mapping adds a social and interactive component to the already powerful process of mind-mapping. Team Mind-Mapping is a terrific way for students to construct, visually display, and later recall their understanding about a topic and its related concepts.

BENEFITS

Students...

...transform the content into a memorable visual/spatial map.

...enjoy the social process of mapping concepts.

...explore contents and connections in great detail.

Getting Ready

Each team receives one large paper and a different colored marker for each teammate.

Step 1 — Teacher Announces Mind-Mapping Topic

The teacher announces the topic to the class. *"We have finished our unit on World War I. In a minute, your team will create a mind map on World War I. Think about everything you learned: the generals, the politicians, the battles, the rationale, the outcome."*

Step 2 — Teammate Writes or Draws Topic

In the center of the paper, one teammate writes or draws the main topic. *"Select one teammate to write 'World War I' in the center of your poster paper and draw a small symbol to represent World War I next to the title."*

Step 3 — Students RoundTable Core Concepts

Students seek consensus on at least four core concepts using RoundTable Consensus. *"Take turns adding core concepts around the main topic. You must receive approval from your teammates before you write or draw your core concept. Come up with at least one each, but you can create as many as your team wants."*

Step 4 — Teams Create Mind Map

In teams, students simultaneously contribute to the mind map by adding subbranches to represent related ideas. Students verbalize the content as they add. Students design and decorate their mind maps using connecting lines, illustrations, symbols, colors, and different sized print. *"Everyone can now add to the team mind map. I want to hear lots of talking. Bounce ideas off your teammates. Share what you're adding and why."*

Team Mind-Mapping

STRUCTURE POWER

Some students love an outline. Others find an outline far too confining: *"How do I show a relation between point ID and IIC1?"* Whereas an outline may satisfy linear thinkers, it frustrates relational thinkers. The mind map is the natural expression of relational thinking. And developing both linear and relational thinking is important. But there is much more to be said in favor of Team Mind-Mapping. Mind-mapping allows easy expression of main ideas, core concepts, and supporting elements—the details. Different students have different cognitive styles. Some are global thinkers, focusing on the forest but sometimes forgetting the trees—they like to come up with the main ideas. Others are analytic thinkers, focusing on the details, but sometimes they focus on the trees and don't see the forest—they like to fill in the supporting elements. Others yet are relational thinkers, focusing on the relationships among concepts—they like to draw the bridges. Because different students bring their unique styles to the team mind map, the resulting map is far richer than any student alone would create. What that means is that all students broaden their picture of the content. Further, most students are visual learners and recall visual information far better than written information. Some students who would hardly remember the content if it were just in words "get the picture" when we do Team Mind-Mapping.

TIPS

• **Model Mind-Mapping.** When introducing mind-mapping to students, model the creation of a simple mind map on the board or using the projector.

• **Sample Mind Maps.** Show students sample completed mind maps and review the various elements of mind maps. You can find some great ones by doing a Google image search on "mind maps."

• **Software Mind Maps.** Software exists for mind-mapping. Teams can build their mind maps on the computer. Because only one student can operate the computer at a time, pairs create more simultaneous interaction than teams. Have partners take turns (RallyTable) adding each new item.

• **Color Key.** Give each student a different color. Students can write a small color key so it is easy to tell who contributed what.

• **Predetermined Core Concepts.** For younger students or to provide more direction to the mind map, the teacher can determine the core concepts students will use. For example, if the map is on the impact of the TV on American society, core concepts could be: political, economic, and social.

IDEAS Across the Curriculum

Mathematics

- Mathematician
- Graphs
- Fractions
- Algorithms
- Math jobs
- Money
- Temperature
- Time
- Volume
- Shapes
- Probability
- Statistics
- Addition
- Subtraction
- Multiplication
- Division

Language Arts

- Book
- Author
- Character
- Grammar
- Letter
- Essay
- Poetry
- Book report
- Prewriting
- Play/skit
- Vocabulary words
- Setting

Social Studies

- President
- Civilization
- Civil War
- Famous women
- Tribe
- Culture
- Careers
- Constitution
- Countries
- Historical characters
- Current events
- Physical geography
- War
- Religion
- Government
- Community
- Discovery
- Martin Luther King, Jr.
- Laws
- Famous speeches

Science

- Invention
- Scientist
- Scientific process
- Ethics
- Genetics
- Nutrition
- Animals
- Birds
- Electricity
- Space
- Gravity
- Magnets
- Natural disasters
- Plants and seeds
- Solar system
- Ocean life
- Dental heath
- Reptiles
- Dinosaurs

Art

- Artist
- Era
- Elements of art
- Mediums

Physical Education

- Tennis
- Soccer
- Volleyball
- Fitness
- Health
- Aerobics
- Weight training

Classbuilding

- Our class
- Our school

Teambuilding

- Our team

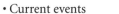

Team Mind-Mapping

VARIATIONS

• **Mind Maps.** Each student creates his or her own mind map. Students share their mind map with a teammate.

• **Thematic Mind Maps.** Give each team a different topic revolving around the class theme. For example, if the class is studying the United States, each team can select a different state. If the class is studying Native Americans, each team can be a different tribe. If the class just read a book, each team can map a different character.

• **RoundTable Consensus.** Instead of simultaneously adding details to the mind map, teams use RoundTable Consensus. Each teammate adds an idea or illustration in turn, but must first receive the team's approval before anything is added. This process is more sequential, but often, this results in a more orderly mind map and requires more consensus seeking.

• **Team Collage.** Teams use magazine and newspaper clippings to build a team collage on a main topic.

• **Share Mind Maps.** Teams share their mind maps using one of these sharing stuctures.
  • Carousel Feedback
  • Carousel Discuss
  • Roam-the-Room
  • Team Inside-Outside Circle
  • Team Rep Interview
  • Team Rep Presentation

#47 Team Word-Webbing

A word web is like a mind map without the visual imagery. Like a mind map, it is a great way to map out core concepts. The team receives a large sheet of paper and each teammate has a different colored pen or marker. The teacher announces the word web main concept. One teammate writes the topic in the center of the sheet and places a box around it. For example, the topic may be "Obama." Teammates take turns writing core concepts around the topic, circling them and connecting them to the topic. For example, main concepts may include biography, election, health care, or wars. Students then add supporting details.

Getting Ready
Each team receives a large sheet of butcher or poster paper and a different color marker for each teammate.

Step 1
Teacher Announces Main Idea

Teacher announces the main idea.

Step 2
Teammate Writes Main Idea

One teammate writes the main idea in the center of the team paper and draws a rectangle around it.

Step 3
Teammates RoundTable Core Concepts

Teammates RoundTable core concepts. Core concepts are written in ovals connected by lines to the main idea.

Step 4
Teammates Write and Draw

The team has a free-for-all. In his or her unique color, teammates write details and draw bridges between related ideas.

THE RAIN FOREST
Team Word-Webbing

Teacher Instructions. Use this sample Rain Forest word web to teach students how to do Team Word-Webbing.

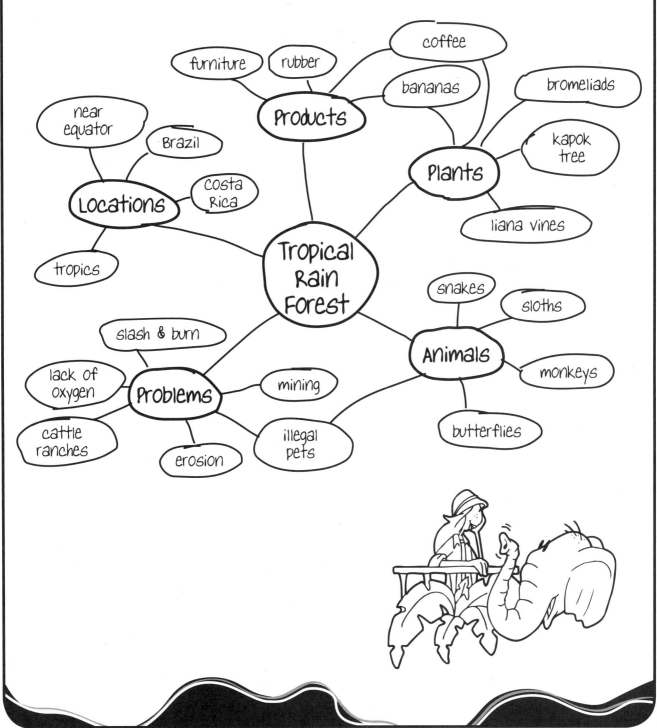

SOURCE: Candler, L. *Exploring the Rain Forest.* San Clemente, CA: Kagan Publishing.

STATE WORD WEB
Team Word-Webbing

Instructions. Fill in the assigned state name and use this form for Team Word-Webbing.

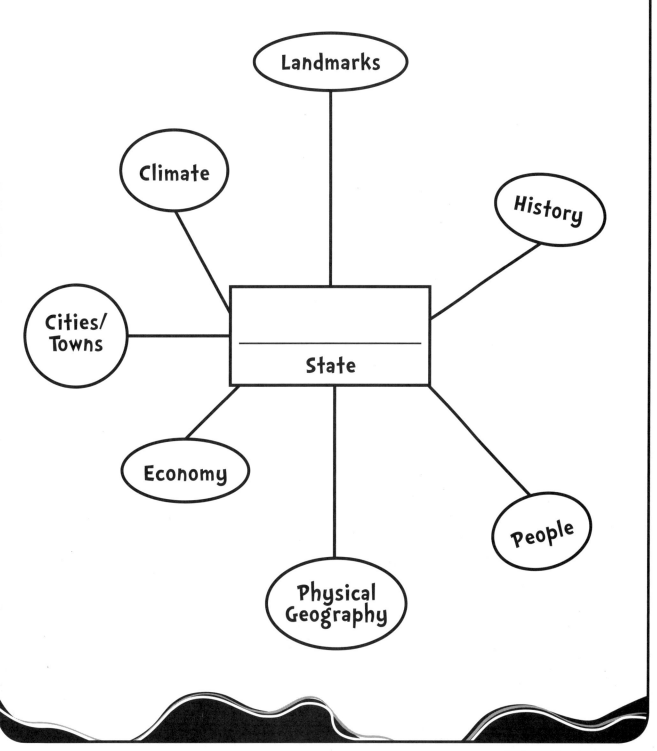

COUNTRY WORD WEB
Team Word-Webbing

Instructions. Fill in the assigned country name and use this form for Team Word-Webbing.

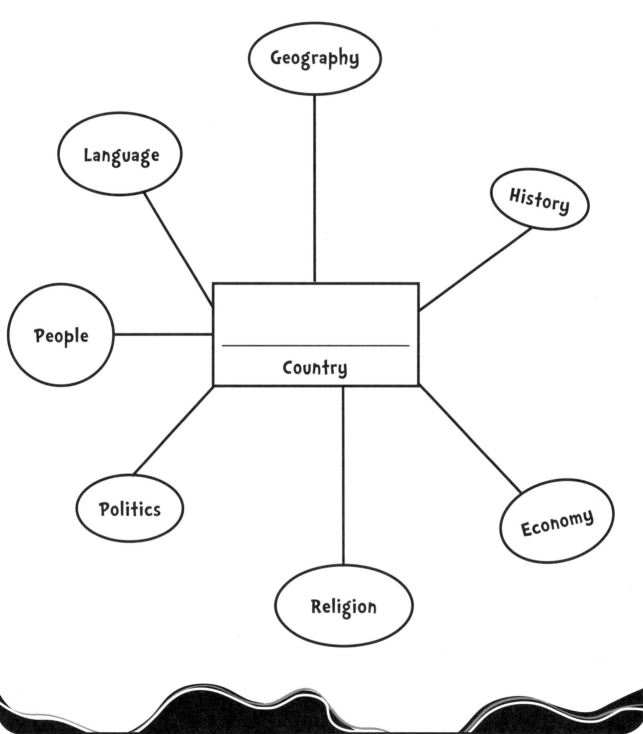

Geography

Language

History

People

Country

Politics

Economy

Religion

ANIMAL WORD WEB
Team Word-Webbing

Instructions. Fill in the assigned animal name and use this form for Team Word-Webbing.

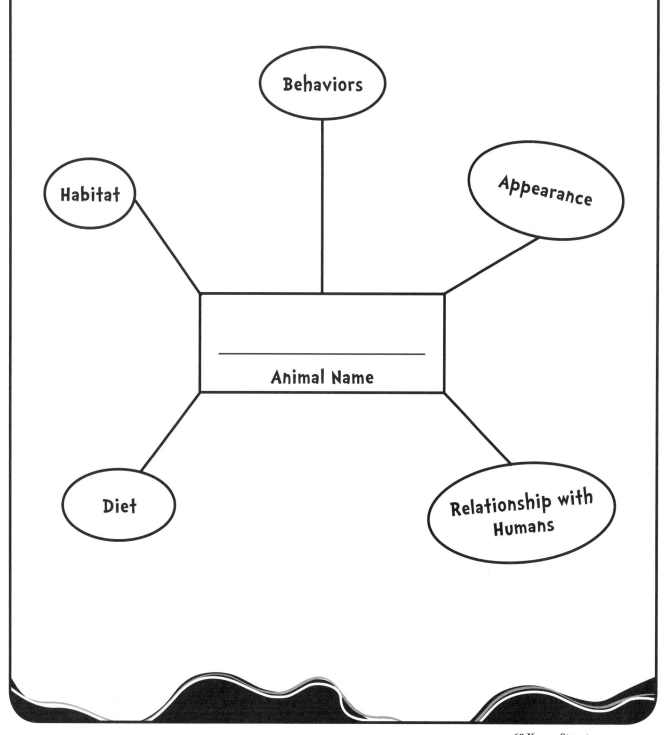

Behaviors

Habitat

Appearance

_____
Animal Name

Diet

Relationship with Humans

CHARACTER WORD WEB
Team Word-Webbing

Instructions. Fill in the assigned character name and use this form for Team Word-Webbing.

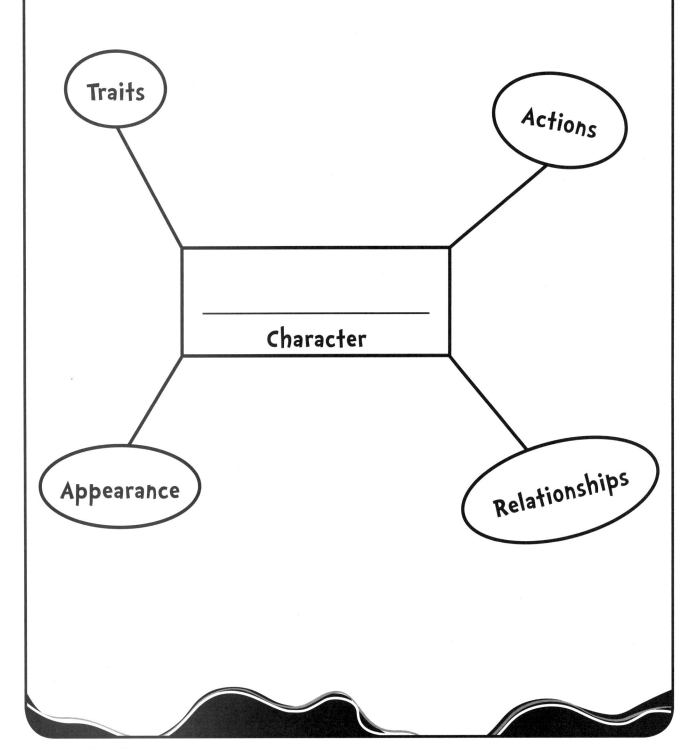

Traits

Actions

Character

Appearance

Relationships

60 Kagan Structures
Kagan Publishing • 800.933.2667 • KaganOnline.com

STORY ELEMENTS
Team Word-Webbing

Instructions. Fill in the assigned story name and use this form for Team Word-Webbing.

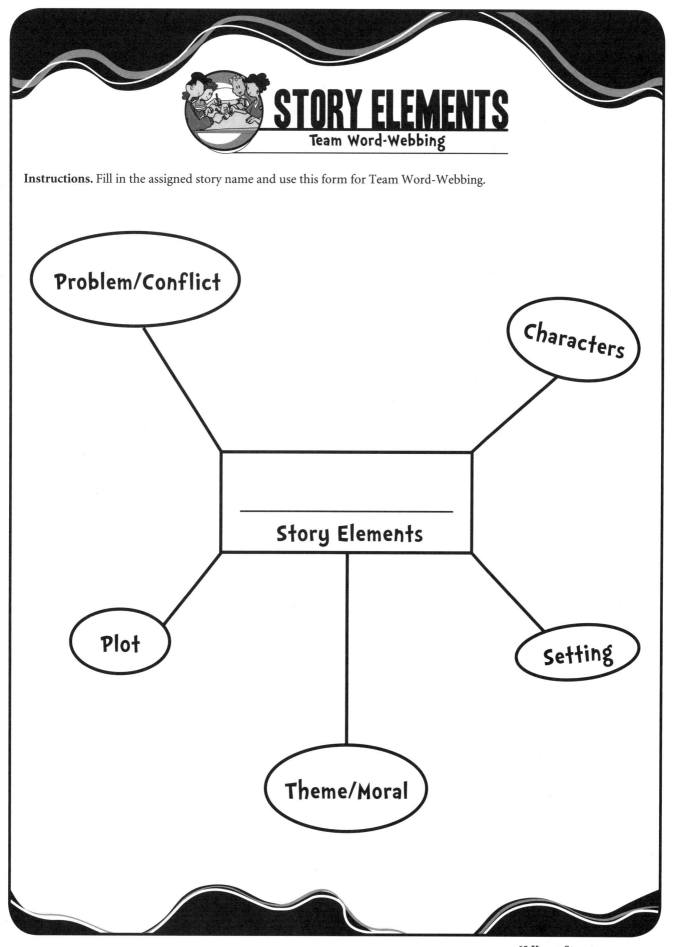

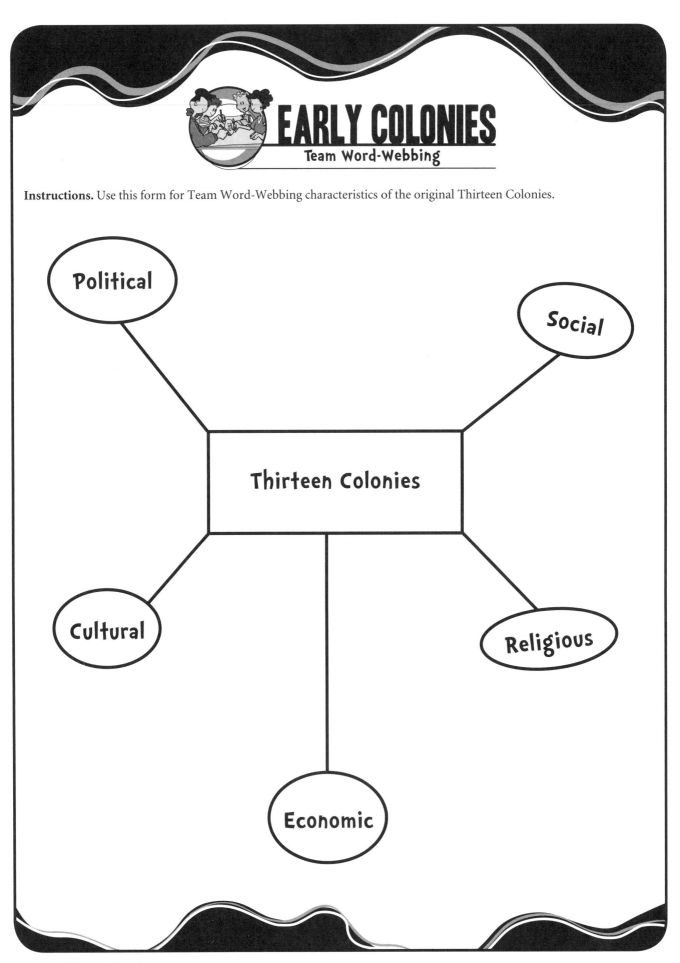

EARLY COLONIES
Team Word-Webbing

Instructions. Use this form for Team Word-Webbing characteristics of the original Thirteen Colonies.

Political

Social

Thirteen Colonies

Cultural

Religious

Economic

TEAM OVERLAP MAP

Structure #48
TEAM OVERLAP MAP

Students work first as a team and then individually to recreate minds maps and literally "fill in the blanks."

STEPS

Getting Ready
Students are given mind maps, or students independently copy a mind map as the teacher draws and explains it.

Step 1
Students Study Maps

When the mind maps are completed, students study their mind maps. They attempt to memorize their mind maps so they can recreate the mind map when it is placed out of sight.

Step 2
Teams Recreate Mind Maps

Students turn their mind maps over or set them out of sight. Teammates work together to redraw the mind map from memory, each drawing with a different color. The team has a time limit for their mind map.

Step 3 — Teams Compare Mind Maps

The team checks the redrawn mind map against a teammate's or the teacher's original.

Step 4 — Teammates Fill in Info

Using RoundTable, teammates take turns filling in the missing information in a bright color.

Team Overlap Map

RELATED STRUCTURE

#49 Overlap Map

Overlap Map is the solo version of Team Overlap Map. Once students have created a mind map, they study it carefully for a specified time period. Their goal is to be able to recreate the map from memory. To study, they practice redrawing it. When time is up, the mind maps are placed out of sight. Students now redraw the mind map from memory. When done, they check the new map against the original. Students fill in any missing details in a bright color.

Getting Ready
Students have created or have been provided a mind map.

Step 1 Students Study Mind Map

Working alone, students study the mind map.

Step 2 Hide Mind Map

The mind map is placed out of sight.

Step 3 Students Redraw from Memory

Working alone, students each redraw the mind map from memory.

Step 4 Check Against Original

Students check their redrawn mind map against the original.

Step 5 Students Revise Their Mind Maps

Students fill in the missing pieces on their mind map in a bright color.

TEAM STAND-N-SHARE

Structure # 50
TEAM STAND-N-SHARE

Teams stand to share their answers with the class.

ONE FACTOR THAT distinguishes cooperative learning from traditional classroom learning is teamwork. In the cooperative class, students do most of their work in teams. Perhaps the greatest advantage of teamwork is that students are much more active in their teams than they could otherwise be in the whole class. But because students work in teams, there is absolutely no reason why teams can't cooperate to share answers and ideas so everyone can benefit from a creative idea or insight. For this exact reason, there are a range of structures for teams to share information with other teams. Team Stand-N-Share is prominent among the team sharing structures.

For Team Stand-N-Share, each team prepares a list of items to share with the class. The list could be instances of foreshadowing in a book, specific examples of a general principle, project ideas, or policy proposals to address a social issue. Any list to which teams may have some different answers can be shared with Team Stand-N-Share. Once each team has its list, all teams stand. The teacher calls on one team to share. The student holding the team list states one idea from the list. The student holding the list on each team adds the idea to his or her team list if it is a new suggestion or checks it off the list if they also had the idea. Teams take turns sharing using either a predetermined sequence or by the teacher calling on each team. The list is rotated within each team after each item is shared. When all of a team's ideas have been shared, the team sits and continues to record additional ideas. When all teams are sitting, all ideas have been shared and each team has an identical list.

Team Stand-N-Share is an efficient process to quickly share ideas among teams so all students may benefit from the ideas generated by other teams. The metacommunication to students is: We may be on different teams, but we are still one class!

BENEFITS

Students...

…share their team's ideas with other teams.

…expand their thinking on a topic.

…generate many items or options as a class.

Getting Ready

Teams prepare a list of items to share with the class. One student in each team holds the team list and the team pen or pencil.

STEPS

Step 1 — Teams Stand

All students stand near their teammates.

Team #1!

Step 2 — Teacher Calls on Team

The teacher calls on one team to share.

Step 3 — Student Shares

The student holding the team list states one idea from the list.

continued

Team Stand-N-Share

Step 4
Add or Check Off Idea

The student holding the list in each team either adds the item to the list if it is a new idea the team didn't have or, if it is already listed, checks it off.

Step 5
Rotate Lists

Teams pass their team lists one teammate clockwise. The teammate with the list is now responsible for adding the next idea, checking it off the list, or sharing if the team is called to share.

Step 6
Teams Sit

The process is continued for each additional item. Teams sit when all their items are shared. While seated they add each new item as it is stated using RoundTable. Team Stand-N-Share is complete when the teacher calls, "*Time,*" or all ideas have been shared.

STRUCTURE POWER

Imagine a class in which each team has generated a list of ideas and the teacher wants teams to hear the ideas of other teams. Without careful structuring, having teams each share a list it has generated might look like this: The teacher calls on one team to share. The high achiever on the team grabs the list and reads it. The teacher calls on the next team, and the high achiever on that team reads that team's list. Next, the teacher calls on a third team. As someone on that team reads its list, half of them are repeats, but it matters little because no one is listening anyway! Several problems are obvious: (1) lack of equal participation in sharing—the high achievers are doing most of the work; (2) lack of listening— there is no accountability for listening; and (3) repetition of items. Team Stand-N-Share eliminates all three problems: Students participate equally in sharing and recording; students listen carefully because they must either add or check off each item; and there is no repetition of items because checked off items are not shared again. With a simple bit of structuring, we transform a boring, repetitious reading of lists into a dynamic sharing with all students listening carefully to the ideas of others. There is power in structures!

TIPS

• **Who Shares?** Use a Student Selector Spinner to randomly pick a teammate number from 1 to 4. Then use a Team Selector to randomly pick a team number. The student selected on the team selected shares his or her list.

• **Generate a List.** For this structure to work well, teams need ideas to share. Use RoundTable, Jot Thoughts, 4S Brainstorming, or any brainstorming structure to generate the list.

Team Stand-N-Share

IDEAS Across the Curriculum

Mathematics
- Ways to represent a number
- Expressions that equal 24
- How to make $1 in coins

Language Arts
- Adjectives that describe a character
- Identify the elements of a story
- Reference books
- Metaphors
- Clichés
- Idioms
- Facts in an article
- Events in a story
- Double-letter spelling words
- Compound words
- Sentences with adverbs
- Proper nouns

Social Studies
- Characteristics of a culture
- A good citizen is someone who…
- Ways to help a friend
- Ways the _____ are like us
- Types of government
- Religions
- Facts about China
- Explorers
- Landforms
- Discoveries
- Examples of change
- Wars
- Battles
- Presidents
- Amendments
- Holidays

Science
- Types of rocks
- Plants
- Ecosystem characteristics
- Things in the ocean
- Things in the rain forest
- Things in space
- Parts of a cell
- Mammals
- Insects
- Elements
- Animals in a habitat
- Appliances that use electricity

Art
- Naming red things
- Artists for a period of time
- Famous artists
- Famous paintings

Physical Education
- Rules of a sport
- Ball sports

Technology
- Parts of a computer
- Programs and what you use them for
- Web sites with important information about…
- Tips for searching
- Uses for a computer

VARIATIONS

- **Teams Post.** To simultaneously share all teams' answers, ideas, or products with the class, the teacher randomly selects a student number. The selected student on each team writes the team's answer or idea, or he or she posts the team's product on a designated area of the board.

- **Continuous Teams Post.** Teams brainstorm ideas or generate a list of responses, sending a different team member up to the board to record each response as it is generated.

RELATED STRUCTURES

#51 Stand-N-Share

Stand-N-Share is a solo version of Team Stand-N-Share. All students stand, each with his or her own list. The teacher selects one student to share. If students already have that idea on their own lists, they check it off. If they don't have it, they add it to their lists. Students sit when each idea on their list is shared. They continue adding new ideas to their lists that classmates share. Stand-N-Share is complete when all students are sitting.

Getting Ready
Students have items to share on a list.

Step 1 Students Stand

Each student stands with his or her own list.

Step 2 Teacher Calls on One Student

The teacher calls on one student to share.

Step 3 Selected Student Shares

The selected student reads one item from his or her list.

Step 4 Add or Check Off Idea

Students add the shared item to their lists if they don't have it or check it off if they do.

Step 5 Students Sit

Each student sits when all of his or her items are shared, continuing to add each new item to his or her list. When all students are seated, Stand-N-Share is complete.

#52 Pair Stand-N-Share

Pair Stand-N-Share is the pair version of Team Stand-N-Share. Students work in pairs to generate a list of ideas. Pairs stand together, and the teacher calls on one pair to share one idea from its list. The other pairs check to see if they have that idea. If they have it, they check it off. If not, they add it. Partners take turns adding each new idea. When all ideas on their list have been shared, they sit down. Once seated, they continue taking turns adding each new idea. When everyone is sitting, Pair Stand-N-Share is complete.

Getting Ready
Pairs have a list of items to share.

 Step 1

Students Stand by Partner

Each student stands next to his or her partner.

 Step 4

Add or Check Off Idea

The student in each pair holding the pair list either adds the item to the list or, if it is already listed, checks it off.

Step 2

Teacher Calls on Pair

The teacher calls on one pair.

 Step 5

Pass List

Students pass their pair list to their partner.

Step 3

Student States Idea

The partner with the list states one idea from the pair list.

 Step 6

Pairs Sit, RallyTable New Items

The process is repeated for each additional idea. Pairs sit when all their items are shared. While seated they add each new item as it is stated using RallyTable. When all pairs are seated, Pair Stand-N-Share is complete.

#53 Whisper It!

The teacher asks a question. Students who know the answer stand. Students who know the answer walk over and whisper the answer to one seated student. Students receiving the answer stand and whisper the answer to another seated student. Students who know the answer continue whispering it to seated students until all students are standing. The teacher then counts down, and then all students simultaneously shout the answer.

Step 1 — Teacher Asks Question

The teacher asks a question.

Step 2 — Students Stand

Students who know the answer stand.

Step 3 — Student Whispers Answer

Students who know the answer walk over and whisper the answer to one seated student.

Step 4 — Another Student Whispers Answer

Students receiving the answer stand and whisper the answer to another seated student.

Step 5 — Process Continues

This process continues until all students are standing.

Step 6 — Students Shout Answer

The teacher then counts down, and then all students simultaneously shout the answer. *"Let me hear the answer in 3...2...1...!"*

Designed by: Chris Hunt

RECORDING SHEET
Team Stand-N-Share

Instructions. Record your team's ideas below. Check off ideas shared with the class, and add any new ideas not on your sheet.

☐ _____
☐ _____
☐ _____
☐ _____
☐ _____
☐ _____
☐ _____
☐ _____
☐ _____
☐ _____
☐ _____
☐ _____
☐ _____

☐ _____
☐ _____
☐ _____
☐ _____
☐ _____
☐ _____
☐ _____
☐ _____
☐ _____
☐ _____
☐ _____
☐ _____
☐ _____

TEAMMATES CONSULT

TEAMMATES CONSULT

Students "consult" teammates, and then they independently solve the problem, answer the question, or record their own ideas.

IN ESSENCE, students collect input from their teammates before they work independently. The type of input depends on what students are working on. If they are working on problem solving, they get input from teammates on how to best solve the problem. For a math example, the word problem asks: "What is half of one quarter of a cup?" Students verbalize how to solve the problem, but no writing and no giving the answer is allowed: *"You multiply fractions, one half times one quarter. You multiply the two denominators to get the new denominator. Then you multiply the two numerators to get the new numerator."* Before students can work the problem through, one student checks to make sure everyone knows how to solve the problem. *"Does everyone know how to write it out and solve it?"* When everyone knows how to solve the problem, they pick up their pencils and paper and work it out or write the answer independently. If they are answering a question, teammates listen to the thoughts and/or beliefs of their teammates before writing their own answer in their own words.

Teammates Consult is a terrific way for students to collect ideas, input, and help from teammates. To make informed decisions and to perform with integrity, collecting input from trusted advisors is a wise process. The president has a cabinet. The CEO has vice presidents. Students have their teammates. Gathering teammates' ideas also promotes verbalization and shared metacognition. Ultimately, though, each student is accountable for his or her own work.

DIFFERENTIATED INSTRUCTION

If Teammates Consult is used for students to take notes in preparation for a test, students are encouraged to take notes in their preferred style—some making illustrations, others writing, yet others creating mind maps or graphic organizers.

BENEFITS

Students...

...verbalize their thinking.

...hear the thinking and problem-solving strategies of teammates.

...receive peer support before independent work.

...remain active participants, accountable to teammates at each step.

...share their ideas and insights about the content.

STEPS

Getting Ready

The teacher prepares a set of problems, questions, or issues to discuss.

Step 1 — Students Number Off

Students number off in their teams from 1 to 4 and place their pens down in the center of the team area or in a pencil cup.

Step 2 — Discussion Leader Reads First Question

Student #1 is the Discussion Leader for the first question. The Discussion Leader reads the first question (or the question may be asked by the teacher). *"What are the differences between the Senate and the House of Representatives?"*

continued

Teammates Consult

Step 3 — Teammates Consult

Starting with the Discussion Leader, teammates RoundRobin their problem-solving strategies or share their ideas. *"One of the biggest differences is the number. There are only two senators per state…"*.

Step 4 — Discussion Leader Checks for Understanding

The Discussion Leader checks with teammates to see if everyone understands, if anyone has any questions, if anyone has anything to add, and if everyone is ready to write or solve the problem independently. At this point, teammates can further discuss the topic if necessary. *"Does everyone have enough information to answer the question? Yes. Then let's write."*

Step 5 — Students Write

Students collect their pens or pencils and write their answers or solve the problem independently with no discussion.

Step 6 — Continue Consulting

When finished writing, teammates place pens or pencils down or in the pencil cup, indicating that they are done. The person on the left of the Discussion Leader becomes the next Discussion Leader for a new round.

Teammates Consult

STRUCTURE POWER

None of us is as smart as all of us. Like the parable of the blind men and the elephant, each of us has our own piece of reality. Only when we put those separate pieces together do we get a fuller picture. One of life's skills is to look at a situation from multiple perspectives before settling on action. Teammates Consult models this process. Students write more thoughtful, informed answers after having listened to multiple points of view. Students reinforce their own thinking and increase their probability of success by verbalizing their thoughts before acting. Teammates Consult is not for test taking; tests are always for individuals performing on their own. Teammates Consult is for learning. Why would we ever want to prevent students from hearing the good ideas of their teammates? By listening to someone who might have a very different opinion than their own, students are forced to sharpen their own thinking. By listening to someone who might offer information they did not have, students make a more informed decision. Teammates Consult has students practice a life skill: Being as informed as possible before drawing conclusions or acting. There is power in making consultation a habit for life!

TIPS

Simple Answers. Teammates Consult does not work with simple computations such as $2 + 2 =$ __. Similarly, it does not not work with one-word answers such as true or false. The problem solving must be of multistep, challenging problems or questions that require elaborate responses or else students will just give the answer rather than exploring the procedure for getting the answer.

Pencil Cups. Place a cup, tub, or mug in the center or each team's table. Students place their pens or pencils in the cup during the consultation period so no one can work on the problem while consultation is in progress. No talking when the cup is empty!

IDEAS Across the Curriculum

Mathematics

Students discuss how to:

• Solve the word problem
• Find the average
• Find the mode
• Multiply the fractions
• Divide the decimal by the whole number

Language Arts

Students discuss how to:

• Write a paragraph
• Write a good topic sentence
• Write a haiku
• Read for comprehension
• Include important details
• Fix the grammar
• Summarize the main point
• Create a mind map on the topic

Social Studies

Students discuss how to:

• Determine the latitude
• Calculate the distance
• Compare the population
• Find where in the chapter it was described
• How to locate necessary information

Science

Students discuss how to:

• Classify animals
• Find the features of Earth
• Characterize rocks or minerals
• Prevent erosion
• Locate planet information
• Define science terms
• Determine inherited traits

Technology

Students discuss how to:

• Program a simple function
• Graph data using a spreadsheet
• Insert a still picture into a video clip
• Download pictures from the Internet
• Convert file formats
• Install a new application
• Organize files
• Lay out a poster in a page layout program
• Draw using Bézier curves

Teammates Consult

VARIATIONS

- **RoundRobin Share.** For written answers, teammates each take a turn reading what they wrote.

- **Showdown Share.** For quick right or wrong answers, teammates simultaneously show their answer boards and verify that everyone got the answer right.

DISCUSSION LEADER ROLE CARD
Teammates Consult

Teacher Instructions. Give each team a Discussion Leader role card to rotate the role during Teammates Consult.

Discussion Leader

❶ Read the question
❷ Lead the discussion
❸ Check for understanding
❹ Rotate the card

Discussion Leader

❶ Read the question
❷ Lead the discussion
❸ Check for understanding
❹ Rotate the card

Discussion Leader

❶ Read the question
❷ Lead the discussion
❸ Check for understanding
❹ Rotate the card

Discussion Leader

❶ Read the question
❷ Lead the discussion
❸ Check for understanding
❹ Rotate the card

SCHOOL DISCUSSION QUESTIONS
Teammates Consult

Teacher Instructions. Select a question from the list below. Have students consult with teammates before writing their own answers to the question.

- Do students have too much, not enough, or just the right amount of homework?

- Are school lunches nutritious? Why or why not?

- Should school start earlier, later, or at the same time it starts now?

- Year-round school is better for students than long summer breaks. Do yo agree or disagree?

- Should all schools have metal detectors for student safety, and why or why not?

- Schools should do away with textbooks, and everything should be in digital format instead. Do you agree or disagree?

- What other classes should schools teach and why?

- Students should be in classes based on their ability level. Do you agree or disagree?

- Students should exercise every day for a healthy body and mind. Do you agree?

TIMED TRAVELERS

Structure # 55
TIMED TRAVELERS

Students travel the room, pairing up with a partner for a specified time interval to discuss questions.

STEPS

Getting Ready
Post multiple discussion questions on the board or give students a handout with multiple discussion questions. Set an interval timer (usually 2 minutes) or prepare to call time after each interval.

Step 2
Partner Reads Question

One partner reads one of the posted discussion questions. For example, *"Why might mathematicians say multiplication is not the same thing as repeated addition?"*

Step 1
Students Pair Up

Students stand up, put a hand up, and high five to pair up with a classmate.

Step 3
Other Partner Responds

The other partner responds.

Step 4 — Partners Switch Roles

After every response, partners switch roles. The partner who shared the last response now asks the next question. For example, *"What does it mean to say division is the inverse of multiplication?"* His or her partner responds. Students stay together and continue to take turns asking and answering questions until time is up.

Step 5 — Continue Pairing

When time is up, partners appreciate each other. For example, *"It's been nice to hear your thoughts."* They shake hands goodbye and put a hand up to find a new partner to share with for the next time interval.

Timed Travelers

9/11 DISCUSSION QUESTIONS
Timed Travelers

Teacher Instructions. Display these questions for students to answer during Timed Travelers.

1. Do you think the United States should have invaded Iraq after 9/11?

2. Should 9/11 be a national holiday? Why or why not?

3. If you were the president of the U.S. and were just informed about the terrorist attacks, what would you do?

4. Is torture ever justified? Why or why not?

5. Do you think a "preemptive" attack is a good idea?

6. Was it a good decision for the U.S. and its allies to invade Afghanistan?

7. If you were a passenger on a hijacked plane, would you confront the hijackers? Why or why not?

8. Why do you think the hijackers chose the World Trade Center, the Pentagon, and the United States Capitol?

9. Should law enforcement agencies have greater power to search people's personal records, search homes and business, and detain suspects in times following terrorist attacks?

10. Was the War on Terror a wise decision? Why or why not?

FUN QUESTIONS
Timed Travelers

Teacher Instructions. Display these questions for students to answer during Timed Travelers.

1 Who is one of your favorite musical groups and why?

2 What do you do with your best friend?

3 What is the worst injury you have had and how did you get it?

4 What is one of the most awkward things you have done?

5 What scares you?

6 What is one of your favorite movies and why?

7 Where is one place you've never been and would love to go? Why?

8 Describe your family.

9 If you could have one superpower, what would it be?

10 If you could only save three things from your burning room, what would you grab?

11 What are three things you want to do before you die?

12 Do you believe in extraterrestrials or aliens? Why or why not?

TOP THREE
Timed Travelers

Teacher Instructions. Display these questions for students to answer during Timed Travelers.

What Are Your Top 3...

...favorite bands?

...favorite songs?

...favorite foods?

...favorite restaurants?

...favorite sports to watch?

...favorite kind of cars?

...favorite movies?

...favorite games?

...favorite colors?

...favorite cartoons?

...favorite flowers?

...favorite desserts?

...favorite vacations locations?

...favorite animals?

TRAVELING STAR

Structure # 56
TRAVELING STAR

Students are randomly selected to stand, travel to another team, and share with their new teammates.

STEPS

Getting Ready
The teacher prepares questions.

Step 1 — Teacher Asks Question

The teacher asks the class a question and gives students 3–5 seconds of Think Time. The question can be a right-or-wrong question: "*Is global climate change provable?*" Or the question can be a thinking question: "*What is one thing we could do as a class to have a positive impact on global climate change?*"

Step 2 — Teacher Calls Number

The teacher calls a student number. One student on each team with the selected number stands. For example, the teacher calls "*Student #2*," and all Student #2s stand.

Step 3 — Teams Beckon

The teacher instructs the seated students to beckon for a standing student to join their team.

Travelers Join New Team

Traveling students join a new team and stand behind the empty chair at that team.

Step 5

Travelers Share

When all teams have a traveler standing behind the empty chair, at a signal from the teacher, travelers share their answers or thoughts with their new teammates, sitting down when finished.

Step 6

Teammates Coach or Praise

For high-consensus questions, teammates praise or, if needed, coach. For low-consensus questions, teammates praise the thinking that went into the answer.

Step 7

Continue Traveling

The teacher asks the next question and calls a new number. Selected students travel to a new team to share.

Traveling Star

VARIATIONS

- **Rotation Pattern.** Traveling students may rotate a specific number through a pre-established pattern, say three teams ahead. This can speed up finding a new team. *"Student #3, please travel two teams to your right."*

- **Random Team Formation.** If more than one round of Traveling Star is used, traveling students are instructed to join a team that their teammates have not already joined. Thus, after three rounds of Traveling Star, new teams have been formed with no students sitting with prior teammates. Students can do an activity in their new random teams.

TURN TOSS

Structure # 57
TURN TOSS

Teammates toss a ball as they generate a list, state answers or ideas, or add to a sequence.

STEPS

Getting Ready
Each team has a small ball, wadded piece of paper, or any item that teammates can toss around.

Step 1
Teacher States Rules

The teacher outlines the rules. *"We are going to play Turn Toss. Here are the rules:*
- *Gently toss the ball underhand.*
- *Be sure the person is ready before tossing it to him or her.*
- *You may not toss the ball back to the person who tossed it to you.*
- *You must toss the ball to a different person each time.*
- *Include everyone equally.*

Step 2
Teacher Announces Topic

The teacher announces the topic. Turn Toss can be used to brainstorm ideas: *"Name a story and the antagonist."* Or Turn Toss can be used to share on any discussion topic: *"On your turn share one thing about yourself."*

Step 3
Start and Toss

A student starts by sharing one idea: *"The Wicked Witch in* The Wizard of Oz.*"* Or he or she starts by sharing on the discussion topic: *"I love to go snowboarding in the winter."* Next, the student tosses the ball to any teammate.

DIFFERENTIATED INSTRUCTION

Young students can be seated and roll, rather than toss, the ball.

Step 4
Catch and Answer

The teammate catches the ball and answers the question or adds to the list of answers: *"The Big Bad Wolf in* The Three Little Pigs."

Step 5
Continue Tossing

Teammates continue responding each time the ball is thrown to them until time is up or until the teacher calls, *"Stop."*

Turn Toss

IDEAS Across the Curriculum

Mathematics

- List odd numbers
- List shapes
- List who might use graphs
- List careers that require math
- List the next number in skip counting
- List the next item in a problem

Language Arts

- List a grammar rule
- Spell a spelling word
- Define a vocabulary word
- List events in a story
- List adjectives
- List proper nouns
- List careers that require writing skills

Social Studies

- List presidents
- List amendments
- List laws
- List events in a period
- List people who make a difference
- List facts about a state
- List countries in Europe

Science

- List mammals
- List minerals
- List landforms
- List careers in science
- List famous inventions
- List things in motion
- List types of weather

FUN LISTS

Turn Toss

Teacher Instructions. Use these topics to play Turn Toss. On their turn, students state one example.

- **Sports**

- **TV Shows**

- **Cartoons**

- **Fruits/Vegetables**

- **Movies**

- **Video Games**

- **Fast Food Restaurants**

- **Good Books**

- **Cereals**

- **Ice Cream Flavors**

- **Candies**

- **Desserts**

- **Drinks**

- **Amusement Park Rides**

- **Weekend Activities**

PARTS OF SPEECH LISTS
Turn Toss

Teacher Instructions. Use these parts of speech to play Turn Toss. On their turn, students can either define the part of speech or provide an example.

- ## Pronoun

- ## Noun

- ## Adverb

- ## Verb

- ## Adjective

- ## Preposition

- ## Interjection

Structure # 58

WHIP

WHIP

Teams in turn quickly state a response.

STEPS

Getting Ready
The teacher asks a question or prepares the sharing topic.

Step 1 — Teacher Announces Topic

The teacher asks a question or tells teams to reach consensus on a word or phrase to share with the class. For example, *"Come up with adjectives or phrases to describe Winston Churchill."* Or, *"State a word or phrase you can use to congratulate a teammate."*

Step 2 — Teams Reach Consensus

In their teams, students reach consensus on what they'd like to share.

Teacher Establishes Sequence

The teacher establishes the order in which teams will share. *"We're going to start with Team #1 and share in order. When the team before you sits down, stand up as a team and call out your word or phrase in unison, and then sit down."*

Step 4 Teams Share

On its turn, the team stands, calls out the response, and then sits down.

Whip

RELATED STRUCTURE

Find One

#59 Individual Whip

The teacher asks a question or asks students to share an idea or response with the class. The teacher describes the sharing sequence. Each student takes a quick turn sharing his or her response.

Step 1 Teacher Asks Question

The teacher asks a question or provides a prompt to which there are multiple short responses. For example, *"What are some examples of insects? See if you can come up with a unique example."*

Step 2 Students Think and Write

Students think about their response and quickly jot it down.

Step 3 Teacher Establishes Sequence

The teacher describes how students will share. *"We'll start with Team #1, Student #1, then Student #2…After everyone on Team #1 shares, Student #1 on Team #2 shares, and so on. Begin!"*

Step 4 Students Share

On their turn, students stand up to share, and then sit down.

Tip

With an Individual Whip, there is a high probability that some students will have the same answer. Here are a few options to handle duplicates:

- Let students restate the redundant answer.
- Have students all stand, then sit if they hear their answer.
- Have students say a quick phrase indicating their answer has already been shared like, *"Pass."*

Structure # 60

WHO AM I?

Structure # 60
WHO AM I?

Students pair up with classmates to ask questions, attempting to discover their secret identity.

STUDENTS EACH have a picture or a word placed on their backs. They try to find out who they are. To do this, they find a partner. Partners look at each other's backs. They take turns asking each other three questions to which their partner may answer only, *"Yes"* or *"No."* After both partners have asked and answered three questions, they each pair with a new partner. Students continue until they can guess who they are. When students guess who they are, their partners move their pictures from their backs to their fronts and congratulate them. Those who have discovered their secret identities become "Helpers." Helpers find a student who still hasn't guessed who he or she is and drop a subtle hint.

Who Am I? develops questioning skills and inductive reasoning. It's a great classbuilder, too, because students are having fun while interacting with many classmates. Students enjoy helping and being helped.

DIFFERENTIATED INSTRUCTION

• Some answers are posted on the board. Students are told, *"Some of you have your secret identity listed on the board, and others do not. Look at the board to get some ideas."* Students who need extra support are given identities that are listed on the board.

• Students can carry paper to record notes.

BENEFITS

Students...

...hone their thinking and questioning skills.

...are actively involved.

...enjoy the guessing game—and knowing a secret their classmates don't yet know.

...learn they need help from others.

...learn questioning strategies and enhance deductive thinking skills.

Getting Ready

The teacher or students make cards. One card is carefully placed on each student's back so students do not see who or what they are.

STEPS

Step 1
Students Pair Up

Students stand up and raise a hand until they find a partner. The pair gives a high five and students lower their hands. *"Find a classmate with a hand up. Give each other a high five and lower your hands."*

Step 2
Partner A Asks Three Questions

Partner A turns around to show Partner B the card on his or her back. Partner A asks Partner B three yes/no questions to discover his or her secret identity. Questions might be: *"(1) Am I a person? (2) Am I a firefighter? (3) Am I a child?"* Partner B answers, *"yes,"* or, *"no"* to each question.

Step 3
Partner B Asks Three Questions

Reverse roles. Partner B now asks three questions and Partner A answers.

Step 4
Students Form New Partners and Continue

Partners shake hands, thank each other, and raise their hands to find a new partner.

Notes

When they are ready and it's their turn, students may make one guess at their identity with each partner. If they choose to make a guess, it counts as one of their three questions. If they are wrong, they keep playing. If they are right, they move their identity card to their front and become a Helper, whispering clues to classmates.

Who Am I?

STRUCTURE POWER

Structure #60

Am I Superman? Am I Einstein? Each of us would like to discover our secret identity! While Who Am I? is a fun, challenge game, it has more power than meets the eye. Students have fun with and learn about the curriculum: To discover which element from the periodic table I am, I discover more about the elements and the arrangement of the periodic table. Students like class more: Students get to move, interact, guess, help, and congratulate each other. Students develop thinking skills: Asking if my name begins with A has only a one in 26 chance of getting a, *"Yes,"* whereas asking if my name begins with a letter that comes before N has a one in two chance of getting a, *"Yes."* Students find they can have fun with every classmate, creating a more inclusive classroom and promoting a more accepting orientation toward individual differences. When students have fun in class, that feeling generalizes to a more positive attitude toward the content, the teacher, and learning. Creating a love of learning is one of the primary goals of schooling—a goal increasingly important as the information explosion and the technological revolution combine to make lifelong learning one of the most important predictors of economic and life success.

TIPS

Student Content. Have students come up with the Who Am I? items (magazines are a good source).

Labels, Name Tags. Use the self-stick labels from a computer or the type used for name tags.

Laminated Pictures. Punch two holes out of a piece of paper and tie yarn through the holes to hang the pictures on students' backs. Pictures will be reusable and easy to switch from the back to the front. You can laminate pictures for reuse. Tape works fine, too.

Placing Pictures. To place pictures on backs, have students form pairs. All Partner As turn their backs to the front of the class while Partner Bs get pictures from the teacher and tape them on Partner As' back. Then Partner Bs turn their backs while Partner As get and place pictures.

Hints. Make sure that Helpers don't give away who the other person is. Work on "subtle" hints. Allow them one hint per person so Helpers continue circulating. For example, if the person is Albert Einstein, the hint may be, *"You are a famous scientist."*

Logical Questions and Guesses. Work with students to ask logical questions that will help narrow down the possibilities. Also help students use their clues to answer correctly. For example, if a student knows he has a female character posted on his back, he need not guess that he is Superman.

60 Kagan Structures
Kagan Publishing • 800.933.2667 • KaganOnline.com

IDEAS Across the Curriculum

Mathematics
- Numbers 1–50
- Geometric shapes
- Amounts of money
- Fractions
- Tools in math (ruler, compass)
- Points on a graph
- Decimals
- Operations

Language Arts
- Characters in a book
- Nouns
- Spelling words
- Parts of speech (verb, adverb, adjective)
- Fairy tales
- Punctuation marks (.!?,)
- Nursery rhymes
- Letters of the alphabet
- Books
- Authors

Social Studies
- Presidents
- States
- Countries
- Places in town (bank, library, school)
- People in community (nurse, police officer, teacher, firefighter)
- Famous people
- Native American tribes
- Culture
- Historical events
- Holidays

Science
- Parts of the solar system
- Plants
- Animals
- Famous scientists
- Sea life
- Endangered species
- Things in a rain forest
- Chemical elements
- Parts of a cell
- Parts of the water cycle
- Tree leaves
- Dinosaurs
- Scientific equipment

Classbuilding
- Other students in the class
- Teachers in the school
- TV programs
- Cartoons
- Items in the room
- Movies
- Movie stars
- Pets
- Restaurants in town
- Desserts
- Sports
- Famous athletes

Who Am I?

MORE IDEAS

Things around School

- Pencil
- Pen
- Crayons
- Calculator
- Desk
- Chair
- Paper
- Book
- Eraser
- Chalk
- Chalkboard
- Projector
- Computer
- Cabinets
- Restroom
- Office
- Drinking fountain
- Classroom
- Library
- Cafeteria
- Auditorium
- Clock
- Window
- Flag
- School bus
- Bike rack
- Field
- Basketball court
- Jungle gym
- Backboard
- Track
- Playground

People in the Community

- Doctor
- Dentist
- Pharmacist
- Lawyer
- Police officer
- Firefighter
- Mail carrier
- Teacher
- Baker
- Butcher
- Grocer
- Clerk
- Salesperson
- Truck driver
- Bus driver
- Delivery person
- Printer
- Astronaut
- Businessperson
- Flight attendant
- Athlete
- Actor
- Musician
- Sanitation engineer
- Electrician
- Plumber
- Gardener
- Construction worker
- Architect
- House cleaner
- Secretary
- Tailor
- Shoemaker
- Interior designer
- Operator
- Server
- Cashier
- Bank teller
- Florist
- Chef
- Farmer
- Pilot

Holidays

- New Year's Day
- Martin Luther King, Jr. Day
- Lincoln's Birthday
- St. Valentine's Day
- Washington's Birthday
- St. Patrick's Day
- Arbor Day
- Easter
- Columbus Day
- Patriot's Day
- Summer Vacation
- Mother's Day
- Flag Day
- Father's Day
- Independence Day
- Halloween
- Thanksgiving
- Chanukah (Hanukkah)
- Christmas Day
- Presidents Day

Fairy Tales and Nursery Rhymes

- "Goldilocks and the Three Bears"
- "Hansel and Gretel"
- "Sleeping Beauty"
- "Dumbo"
- "Peter Pan"
- "Humpty Dumpty"
- "The Three Little Pigs"
- "Little Red Hen"
- "Jack and the Beanstalk"
- "Snow White and the Seven Dwarfs"
- "Puss and Boots"
- "The Elves and the Shoemaker"
- "Little Jack Horner"
- "Old Mother Hubbard"
- "Three Blind Mice"
- "Three Little Kittens"
- "Rapunzel"
- "Beauty and the Beast"
- "Jack and Jill"
- "Little Miss Muffett"
- "Mother Goose"
- "Frog and Toad"
- "Pinocchio"
- "Rumpelstiltskin"
- "Cinderella"
- "Aladdin"
- "The Little Mermaid"
- "Three Billy Goats Gruff"
- "Little Red Riding Hood"
- "The Little Red Hen"
- "The Ugly Duckling"
- "The Emperor's New Clothes"
- "Chicken Little"
- "The Princess and the Pea"
- "Little Jack Horner"
- "Jack Sprat"
- "Sing a Song of Sixpence"
- "Mary, Mary, Quite Contrary"
- "Little Boy Blue"
- "Little Bo Peep"

VARIATIONS

• **Who Are We?** Students can play Who Am I in pairs or in teams. Students travel in pairs or in teams to find out who they are. They take turns asking the questions. This variation makes the game easier because fewer pictures are used. To make sure partners or teammates don't see their own picture, students put their arms around each other's shoulders.

• **What Am I?** Inanimate objects may be used.

• **Where Am I?** Places may be used.

• **When Am I?** Historical dates and events may be used.

• **Identity Storehouse.** When a student discovers who he or she is, instead of becoming a Helper, he or she can visit the identity storehouse and have a new identity placed on his or her back.

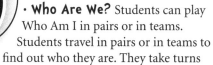

Teacher Instructions. Use these topics to create Who Am I? cards for your class.

- **Celebrities**
- **Athletes**
- **Famous People in History**
- **U.S. Presidents**
- **Animals**
- **States**
- **Careers**
- **Cartoon Characters**

NOTES

NOTES

NOTES

NOTES

NOTES

NOTES